Y0-DRY-980

HIS HOLINESS, POPE PAUL VI
after perusing this book, sent author His
PATERNAL APOSTOLIC BLESSING

Segreteria di Stato
di Sua Santita

No. 76171

DAL VATICANO July 17, 1966

    THE SECRETARIAT OF STATE OF HIS HOLINESS at the gracious command of the Sovereign Pontiff, acknowledges receipt of the volume, "The Last World War and the End of Time", which Mr. Emmett Culligan recently placed at His disposal.

    The Secretariat of State is directed to give expression to the Holy Father's warm appreciation of the loyal sentiments of filial homage which inspired this presentation, and to convey to the donor, as a pledge of copious rewarding heavenly favours, the Paternal Apostolic Blessing of His Holiness.

The Last World War and THE END OF TIME

By

EMMETT J. CULLIGAN, K.S.G., K.M.

TAN BOOKS AND PUBLISHERS, INC.
Rockford, Illinois 61105

By decree of the Holy Office in Rome *(Acts of the Apostolic See:* December 26, 1966) books on prophecy and apparitions no longer require an imprimatur.

Copyright © 1975 by TAN Books and Publishers, Inc.

Originally published by Emmett J. Culligan in 1950 and later by Circle Books, Culligan Books, Culligan Publications, Inc. and Elbee Press.

ISBN: 0-89555-034-2

PRINTED AND BOUND IN THE UNITED STATES OF AMERICA

TAN BOOKS AND PUBLISHERS, INC.
P.O. Box 424
Rockford, Illinois 61105
1981

CONTENTS

	Page
DEDICATION	iii
FOREWORD — REV. JEROME PALMER, O.S.B.	viii
AUTHOR'S FOREWORD	xii
PART ONE — THE WORLD OF TODAY	1
CHAPTER 1 — THE LAST WORLD WAR	1
PART TWO — POLITICAL DANGERS	9
CHAPTER 2 — THE CAUSE OF ATHEISM	11
CHAPTER 3 — MAJOR VINCENT HARRINGTON	33
CHAPTER 4 — THE GREAT BETRAYAL	39
PART THREE — MORAL DANGERS	53
CHAPTER 5 — SATAN IN OUR DAY	55
PART FOUR — THE DAY OF THE LORD	63
CHAPTER 6 — THE DAY OF THE LORD	65
CHAPTER 7 — A LETTER FROM FATHER M. RAYMOND, O.C.S.O., TRAPPIST AUTHOR	71
CHAPTER 8 — WE ARE LIVING IN THE TIME OF THE APOCALYPSE	75
CHAPTER 9 — SECOND COMING OF CHRIST AS TOLD IN THE BIBLE	88
CHAPTER 10 — THE COMING OF THE DREADFUL ANTICHRIST	99
CHAPTER 11 — THE END OF THE WORLD? NO, NOT YET	113
CHAPTER 12 — PROPHETS AND PROPHECIES	123
CHAPTER 13 — DON'T RISK HELL	139
PART FIVE — MARY OUR HOPE	149
CHAPTER 14 — MARY OUR HOPE	151
CHAPTER 15 — TRIUMPHANT PEACE	175
CHAPTER 16 — A MESSAGE TO OUR CHILDREN	189
EPILOGUE	195
CHAPTER 17 — OUR EIGHT YEARS IN THE MOUNTAINS	197

I have read the book, "The Last World War and End of Time," by Emmett Culligan, a fine Catholic author who really sees the conditions of the world, as well as in the church, in this era. To me, after the Bible, this book is the most serious and revealing. Reading it has given me the greatest enthusiasm to learn more and more about this era. I do really believe, as the author does, that it reveals what is taking place in every day of our lives. A thinking person cannot help seeing the reality that we are truly living in a time when many prophecies of the old and new testament are being fulfilled.

Mr. Guy Giorgio
Forest Park, Illinois

PRINTING HISTORY

First .... August, 1950
Second .... April, 1952
Third .... November, 1952
Fourth .... April, 1953
Fifth......................... July, 1953
Sixth .... October, 1953
Seventh .... July, 1954
Eighth .... November, 1956
Ninth—Revised .... May, 1966
Tenth..................... January, 1967
Eleventh .... February, 1970
Twelfth .... March, 1973
Thirteenth .... November, 1975
Fourteenth................. March, 1981

THE REASON FOR THIS BOOK

I was born a Roman Catholic. All my ancestors for 1400 years have been Catholics. Not one of my forefathers gave up his Catholic faith. I believe nothing matters other than saving my own soul; and nothing is more important than helping others save their souls.

THIS BOOK AIMS AT SAVING SOULS

The six Popes of the Twentieth Century have called upon the laity, again and again, to participate in the Royal Priesthood. Catholic lay people have a right and duty to exercise the apostolate which stems from their very union with Christ the Head. In writing this book, the author has attempted to do so. We, laity, sons of God, and thereby members of the most kingly of all royal families, should speak out to denounce worldwide atheism that is bringing darkness over the whole earth.

DEDICATION

This book is affectionately dedicated by the author to the Blessed Mother of God under the title *Empress of the Americas* as Pope Pius XII titled our Lady of Guadalupe. It is meant to be an appeal to the Sorrowful and Immaculate Heart of Mary in behalf of those most in need of divine mercy.

This colored print was copied from the original image that the Mother of God gave to the people of America in the year 1531.

OUR LADY'S GIFT TO THE AMERICAS

A miraculous portrait of the Mother of God hangs above the main altar in the Basilica of Our Lady of Guadalupe. It was painted with brushes from another world on coarse maguey or cactus fiber, and after over 400 years this heavenly portrait is as fresh and bright today as when it was miraculously done on the grass like cloth of an early American Indian.

Unless one has been part of the throng at the Shrine of Guadalupe he cannot grasp the marvellous effect on the continent of North America of a miracle that started in 1531 on the hillside of Tepeyac, now in the outskirts of Mexico City, and continues a miraculous proof of our Lady's love to this day. The 1500 pilgrims from a single village, walking sixty miles in four days, to thank our Lady for her interest was but one of countless such testimonials in December 1965, when the author was privileged to join their number and there formally to dedicate this little book to our Mother under the title given her by Pope Pius XII, *Empress of the Americas.*

From prehistoric times estimated to be during the eighth millennium (before Christ[1]) the Indians in the region are now known to have been a religious people. The Toltecs, whose traditions date back at least to the third millennium B.C., conquered the valley of Mexico in the beginning of the tenth century of our era. The Aztecs, led by Moctezuma, took over about the middle of the fifteenth century. From then on Cortez and the Spanish conquistadores brought Mexico into modern history. Ten years after that conquest the miracle of the image occurred.

The Spanish brought Christianity, and while today we deprecate their destructive and piratical methods, we must give them credit for firmly establishing Christianity among the natives.

They were divinely assisted, when in seven years after the miraculous image appeared, eight million Indians applied for

---

[1]Bernal Ignacio, *Mexico before Cortez, Art, History, and Legend,* Dolphin Books, Garden City, New York, p.7.

baptism at the various Franciscan missions scattered throughout the region. The Spaniards tore down temples to the numerous gods and built fantastic churches, whose canvases and statues and gold defy an assessor's talent today.

On December 9, 1531, an Indian, Juan Diego, stood at the foot of Tepeyac, a hill 130 feet high, and heard unearthly music from its top. When he looked up to the spot whence it seemed to come, he saw a brilliant cloud. The music ceased and he heard himself called by name: "Juanito, dear Juan Dieguito." He climbed the hill, a steep climb as anyone who makes it today will testify, and there he saw a beautiful maiden. So brilliant was her appearance that stones and trees and earth seemed to turn to precious stones.

She spoke to him affectionately. "My dear son, whom I love tenderly, I wish you to know that I am the Virgin Mary, Mother of the true God, Giver and Maintainer of life, Creator of all things, Lord of heaven and earth, Who is in all places. It is my ardent wish that a temple be erected to me here where I can manifest the compassion that I have for the natives, and for all who solicit my help in their work and their affliction, where I shall see their tears and listen to their pleadings, to give them comfort and ease.

"In order that my wish may be fulfilled, you must go to Mexico, to the house of the Bishop, and tell him that I sent you, that it is my desire to have a temple built for me here. Tell him what you have seen and heard, and be sure that I shall be grateful to you for doing what I ask. I shall make you happy and reward you for the service you will render to me. My son, you have heard my wish. Go in peace."

The Bishop listened but did not believe the story. He asked Juan to return later and tell him more. Later that afternoon Juan again visited the hill and again saw the apparition. He begged that someone else be sent whom the Bishop might more readily believe.

When on December 10 Juan again called on the Bishop, his sincerity moved the prelate and he asked that some sign or token of the heavenly nature of the message be given.

Mary again appeared to Juan on the hill that same day and promised the requested sign on the morrow.

The following day Juan was detained by the serious illness

of his uncle and thought he should forego the visit with our Lady. She, however, met him again on his way, promised to cure his uncle, and bade the Indian to climb up to the hilltop where she had previously met him and there to cut flowers from the many he would find there.

Juan was perplexed. He knew no flowers grew on that hill, but he obeyed and was richly rewarded, for he found roses of unearthly fragrance and beauty. (At that time roses had not yet been introduced into Mexico.) He brought them to Mary, who herself arranged them and tied the corners of his tilma in a knot behind his neck to hold them. "This is the sign that you are to take to the Lord Bishop," she said. "It will convince him so that he will most enthusiastically comply with my request to erect a hermitage for me in that place. Now, my son, listen carefully to what I tell you. You are my ambassador worthy of confidence. Do not let anyone see what you are carrying; do not unfold your mantle until you are in his presence. Tell him what I have just now commanded you to do."

When after a long period of waiting Juan was greeted by the Bishop, he opened his tilma and the roses fell onto a bench. In that moment the incomparably beautiful picture or image of the Virgin Mary on the coarse tilma was revealed for the first time to the eyes of men.

The Bishop and his staff fell on their knees and soon arranged to construct the great shrine on the spot of the apparitions.

The miraculous picture could never have been painted by human artist on the coarse material, a cactus fibre, with no preparation whatsoever. It cannot be done today and certainly could not have been done by an unschooled Indian in the sixteenth century. The color of the rough material is almost that of unbleached linen. Two pieces of the material are sewn together, but the seam, which is visible in the middle, in no way affects the picture, since our Lady graciously depicted her head inclined to one side.

The color of the skin and hair is that of the natives, and the cloth that covers her head and body resembles the gala dress of the Aztec princess. It is greenish blue, adorned with forty-six stars of eight points and with a golden border of finest gold.

The embroidered design visible on the tunic is not worked into the material. It is like lace over the tunic. Artists of worldwide repute are baffled by the ability of the material to show the colors, to withstand the exposure for over four hundred years (for one hundred years without even the protection of a glass covering). There are other marvels in this picture which authors describe but which space does not permit describing here. Pope Benedict XIV established the feast and Mass of our Lady of Guadalupe in 1764. Mindful of the papal sanction given by twenty popes since 1660, Pope Leo XIII gave special recognition to the marvel, and Pius XII give Mary the title *Empress of the Americas*.

It is to our Lady of Guadalupe that the author dedicates his book, hopeful that the faith and love inspired in the Mexican Catholics will not be confined by national boundaries, but reach all Americans everywhere.

A small booklet "America's Treasure" explaining the whole story of Guadalupe, with pictures in real colors, is available from Helen Behrens, Apartado 26-732, Mexico, D.F.

REV. JEROME PALMER, O.S.B.

FOREWORD

In THE LAST WORLD WAR Sir Emmett Culligan, K.S.G., has taken the almost universal feeling of our day — that the world is in serious crisis — and has traced this feeling to some definite causes, some economic, some political, but ultimately all spiritual. What James Carlton Hollenbeck has called "the uneasiness of today, . . . the consciousness that we are passing through a very grave crisis of civilization,"[1] is here found to be the realization that man's departure from the moral law must inevitably bring some kind of retribution.

"Humanity, in its waking hours, sees the grim spectacle of a long black night descending upon the world, of one nation after another passing under the yoke of the new slavery, and the vast majority of the human race threatened with reduction to serfdom and that of mere coolies."[2]

---
[1] Hollenbeck, James C., *The Super-Deceiver on the World Horizon*, Advance Publications, Chicago 13, Ill., p. 7.
[2] *Ibid.*

If man were left entirely to his own resources the outlook would indeed be hopeless. What fatalists would see in the ever-worsening condition, Sir Emmett sees as the darkness before the dawn, the prelude to the "Triumphant Peace" promised at the Cova da Iria in Portugal half a century ago.

Perhaps the shadows that have darkened the earth for decades when they first began to form were not unnoticed by sensitive men. One cannot but be impressed by Heinrich Heine and his frightening description of our day, written one hundred twenty years ago.

"Christianity has moderated the brutishness of the Germanic races who fought for the mere love of battle. When the cross of Christianity is broken the long smouldering ferocity of ancient warriors will again blaze up. The Christian talisman is rotten with decay and will soon crumble and fall. Then the ancient gods will rub the dust out of their eyes and will arise from dismantled ruins. Then Thor, with his colossal hammer, will leap up and break into a thousand pieces the Gothic cathedrals. A drama will be enacted in Germany that will make the French Revolution seem a harmless idyll.

"When revolution begins to sweep the earth," he wrote in 1842, "we shall see the emergence of the most appalling of all the antagonists who ever stood forth to do battle against the existing order. The antagonist has not as yet made its appearance, but will emerge under the term "Fascism," and will be the most redoubtable adversary who has ever marched against the existing order. War will be merely the first act of the great drama and will be no more than a prologue. The second act will be the European revolution, the world revolution, the immense combat between the have-not's and the have's."[1]

The two thousand years in which Christianity has been at work redeeming the world, not always as thoroughly or as rapidly as we should like, have been centuries of conflict and disappointment and apparent failures. Yet slowly, and surely, the cross has been carried from Jerusalem to Greece and Rome, to all Europe, then to North and South America, to Africa and to Asia. If evil seems at times to move like a juggernaut against

---
[1] Heinrich Heine.

the forces of good, we invariably find when the dust of battle has settled that the Cross stands proudly over conquered territory.

This is the story of THE LAST WORLD WAR. Wars are not entirely caused by the machinations of politicians, though they are usually occasioned by them. The causes lie deeper. Man's insubordination to God, man's defiance of supernatural law, is but the repetition of the first man's disobedience. And so sin is at the bottom of all wars. You and I have had a share in causing the sufferings of countless exiles as they trekked across Europe, Jews seeking their ancient homeland, Poles and Austrians seeking asylum under the statue of Liberty. The unhappy Cubans in flight from their tyrant-dictator are but paying the price in God's way for the sins of mankind. When these sins are curbed, when sinners turn again to God, wars will cease and we will have the triumphant peace so ardently sought by men today.

The benighted demonstrators against Vietnamese wars, the beatniks cluttering up the Spanish Steps, all know, indeed, what is wanted — peace. But they have not learned that the method is to stop sinning, to practice virtue. This is the thesis of Sir Emmett's book. God speed it on its way as a real contribution to peace among thinking people.

Rev. Jerome Palmer, O.S.B.

Oceanside, California, December 12, 1965

AUTHOR'S FOREWORD

How narrow the gate and close the way that leads to life! And few there are who find it. MATT. 7:14

If at times, as you read on in this book, the tone of writing appears unduly severe, attribute this to my contacts with closed minds that should not be closed to the subject of this writing. What is said is well supported by approved apparitions of Our Lord and His Mother to saintly people for the purpose of helping all men and women find the narrow road that leads to their personal salvation. This book is intended to be a lantern light at the side of that narrow road. It is only because souls may be lost for all eternity that I write at all. Our world today is not a Christian world. It has become a secular and a pagan world. Most followers of Christ have become conditioned in their relation with one another by the effect of four centuries of selfish, Godless thinking. In our present age, there is a systematic effort by great numbers of present day pagans, who want only materialism, to destroy Christian morality and eliminate Christian culture.

It is obvious to thinking people that Western civilization has been advancing through the 20th century toward some final climax that may bring on its end. We see signs of moral decay throughout the whole world. So significant is all this, that American people are convinced that a momentous heaven-sent crisis may soon be here. This consciousness has developed a widespread desire to come close to God. It has brought on a religious revival among Christian people of all faiths. There are Americans not content to obtain heaven at a low price, seeking nothing less than sainthood through Christian perfection, and obtaining it through prayer and penance.

Non-Catholic Americans are turning to their Catholic neighbors to discuss spiritual matters and get comfort from what Catholics can tell them. Catholics should know what is to come. The Mother of God has appeared time and time again to warn that men on earth must stop offending her Divine Son. In 1917 in Portugal, she came six times and told us that if man did not change his ways a second world war would come on to be followed with the scourge of World Communism. She promised, however, "In the end — there will be peace."

This book gives one Catholic layman's interpretations of what he expects will come. I consider it a duty in charity to do what I can to prepare Christian people for the coming of a cataclysm which may be nothing less than a final warning for all men throughout the whole world. It is my hope that this book will help drive away apathy and complacency.

An apocalyptic message will never be universally popular, but it is in order in these times. I am aware that it is a sensational topic on which to write and that I will be subject to innumerable criticisms on that account. I expose myself knowingly and willingly to criticisms, for I passionately believe all that is said in this book. I believe it so confidently that I dare publish it for others to share with me. If I am right in my belief that a great era of world peace and the triumph of the Church will follow this cataclysm, surely all Christians should be alerted. It is the enactment of the parable of the grain and the cockle which I believe is near at hand. "One will be taken and one will be left." (Matthew 24:40.)

WHY THIS BOOK WAS WRITTEN

As the Korean War got under way in 1950 I undertook to determine for my own private information the real cause of these terrible world-wide conflicts. I wanted to know what was back of World Wars. The more I read, and the further I inquired of Christian thinkers, many of them in monasteries and convents, the tragic, diabolical causes of these wars became evident.

I outline these causes in these pages. One of the main reasons for doing so is to inform my wife and our seven adult children, their wives and their husbands and our 35 grandchildren, so the Culligan clan can prepare to calmly meet the days immediately ahead, with faith, with hope, and with courage. It is God's will that I so inform them.

The first printing of this book carried a notation: "A Private Printing — For Family Only." However, even with this limitation it was read by many people.

There are those who know much about the contents of this book who maintain that the information should not be broadcast for fear it might frighten people. It will frighten people. It frightened me; but it also brought me closer to God. It gave me comfort, too, to learn for the first time since 1914, what is back of world wars; that the terrific military struggles now underway, in 1965, throughout the whole world are not just another world war, but rather a dramatic crisis of the great Biblical drama of Christianity that has been running for over nineteen centuries. Our apocalyptic times are foretold time and again in the Bible. Many friends, some of them not of my own faith, who are true Christian American neighbors, have urged that I make this information available to all faiths, and have assured me that it will give men and women great satisfaction to know what is really back of these diabolical wars. I am told it will aid in establishing a united Christian front to meet our common Godless enemy — Communism. *And I am told it will save souls.* It was this assurance that prompted me to publish it. If by so doing it saves but one soul from the fires of hell, I will be grateful during all eternity.

It is my hope that this book may be helpful to many fine Americans who have been unconscious victims of modern materialism, and that in some cases, because of the stresses and strains they were called upon to bear, God was crowded out of their lives. I have consideration for the opinion of all Christian people, and especially those whose faith differs from mine.

The reader's belief in the revelations that have been made to saintly mystics and referred to in this book, is not required by the Church even when the Church formally approves them. By giving approbation to such revelations, the Church only intends to declare that nothing is to be found in them contrary to faith and morals, and that they can be accepted without danger and even with advantage.

After being assured that there is nothing in this book contrary to Catholic truth, it was published as the opinion of and by no other authority than that of one Catholic layman who personally is convinced that world events are rapidly leading to the most dramatic happening in all the history of man, and that all Christian people should know this in advance.

The writer is by no means alone in believing as he does regarding the days through which we are passing. Theological students while in seminaries years ago were told by their archbishop to prepare for the great persecution of the Church during their lifetime. Most nuns in convents know that trouble is now here. Great numbers of lay people, even without benefit of any special reading, are convinced that our civilization is ready to collapse. But there is a strange apathy everywhere. Few people will talk on this subject; much less are they prepared to face it. In this I believe, they are wrong. Christians should look upon these last days with joy. What is to happen is God's way of bringing our disordered times to an end. If the events described herein are about to occur surely all Christians should look upon these critical days without fear. What is to happen is God's way of bringing our disordered times to order. If the events described herein are about to occur surely all Christians should know this in advance. If the saintly mystics who have been warning us are wrong, they can be wrong only as to time, as Christ gave the same kind of messages to His apostles. In reading what these seers (most of them saints) foresaw, and in contemplating the coming of these biblical events no one can suffer harm, but only good can result. It will make us more God conscious. It will make us realize with more certainty that He made us for one purpose only, which is to be with Him forever. The world comes to an end for 200,000 people on earth every day. If in His wisdom He is about to speed up this process for thousands more, why should any Christian fear?

ARMAGEDDON AT OUR DOOR

"Men since the beginning of time have sought peace. Various methods through the ages have been attempted to devise an international process to prevent or settle disputes between nations. From the very start workable methods were found in so far as individual citizens were concerned, but the mechanics of an instrumentality of larger international scope have never been successful. Military alliances, balances of power, leagues of nations, all in turn failed, leaving the only path to be by way of the crucible of war. The utter destructiveness of war now blocks out this alternative. We have had our last chance. If we will not devise some greater and more equitable system, ARMAGEDDON WILL BE AT OUR DOOR. The problem basically is theological."

— General Douglas MacArthur

These words were spoken by the great American General as he accepted the surrender of Japan, August 15, 1945, and before Congress, April 19, 1951.

GENERAL DOUGLAS MacARTHUR

Part 1

The World Today

Chapter 1

The Last World War

The world has too many men of science, too few men of God. — GEN. OMAR N. BRADLEY, 1952.

At noon, on the second day of August, in the year 1914, I came in to dinner at our farm near Maurice, Iowa, and handed the mail to the father of the family who operated the farm. He was an elderly Hollander, over from Europe but a few years. The paper carried the terrible headline: "KAISER WILHELM GOES TO WAR." The old man said: "It has finally come," and, turning to me, he said: "Young man (I was 21 years old), you will be an old man before this war ends." How right he was. I am an old man now of 72 years, and it still goes on.

The First World War cost the world 32 million casualties and 336 billion dollars. The Second World War took nearly as many lives, but cost a great deal more in property and money. One participant alone, the United States, spent in excess of one trillion dollars.

And now the last world war has seemingly begun. The battle lines are forming, the men are being called up and trained, and whether atomic weapons are used or not, when this war finally ends there will be no *will* ever to go to war again. One wonders whether there will be enough of mankind left on the earth ever to consider another war. I believe that just as a flood can cause animals hostile to one another by nature and instinct to seek safety side by side on a drifting log, so the horrible cataclysm implied in another war will drive the survivors to huddle together so closely that if they do not form the one fold under the one Shepherd, at least they will seek together to avert any further disasters.

Each of the three phases of World War have indicated the wandering of the race from the principles of Christianity. World

War One grew out of nationalistic pride and instead of the mighty empire envisioned by the perpetrator, left the shambles of devastation that pride always produces. The Second World War was to promote the despicable *Uebermensch* or Superman philosophy, and left its two most daring promoters dead, one hanging by his heels alongside his mistress, the other shot to death in his bunker by his own pistol. The Third World War, now already in probing stages throughout the world, is the work of atheism. The perpetrators of it are bent on disproving all religion. They would deny glory to God and thus deprive us of Peace to men of good will.

The United States of America until 1932 was always a Christian country, founded by Christian men, who wrote down their Christian principles in a Declaration of Independence in a protest against the anti-Christian rulers of the old world. These Christian men set about to build a Christian nation. One of their first acts was to make religious medals of our coins by engraving thereon an Act of Faith: "In God We Trust." On this Christian foundation there was built the greatest nation the world has ever seen.

American culture until recent years has always been traditionally Christian. American government and Democracy were based on cognizance of God. In late years, however, the very foundations of our great nation have been threatened by those who would dethrone God; by those who would destroy the very concept of God in the minds of our people. The destruction of belief in God, and the destruction of traditional American Christian culture, meant the destruction of America as a nation — great, and noble, and free.

After 1932, attempts were made to modify, or to drop, many of the principles outlined in our national Constitution; the Supreme Court of the United States was "packed"; bureaucratic government was set up and the breaking down of our great Republican Democracy was under way.

The human race is divided into two parts. In one division are the friends of God; these constitute the forces of Good or are the Constructionists who built Christian civilizations. In the other division are the enemies of God; these constitute the force of Evil or are the Destructionists who have been actively endeavoring to tear down that which the forces of Good have built.

The people of the world, regardless of what country they live in, are taking sides in this great struggle. Great numbers of those who should be among the forces of Good are actively assisting in the destruction of the Christian way of life.

The forces of Good have as their leader Jesus Christ. The forces of Evil have as their leader none other than Satan, who has behind him the Communist armies of Russia and China and their allies. They all have the Communist philosophy of destruction.

These Destructionists have received great assistance from some of our leaders in the United States, who are sympathetic to their cause, who caused to be sent to Russia an amazingly large amount of armament and money, which now forms the very foundation, not only for arms, but also the know-how to duplicate American craftsmanship to carry on another world war. These were sent in spite of the previous bloody record of Stalin, the modern Nero, who ordered that millions of civilians be murdered for no other reason than that they were among the forces of Good, and refused to deny Christ. Here is a partial list of the materials misguided leaders of our own dear country sent to Russia. Some of these gifts are now in Asia, being used to kill our own sons. Our own injured boys have had bullets removed from their bodies bearing the familiar trademark — "Made in U.S.A."

We gave Stalin for his Communist armies, 14,450 fighting and pursuit planes; 3,000 bombers; 7,000 tanks; 3,200 armored scout cars; 2,200 ordnance semi-vehicles; 52,000 jeeps; 363,000 trucks; 35,000 motorcycles; 8,200 anti-aircraft guns; 135,000 submachine guns; 343,000 tons of explosives; 105 submarine chasers; 195 torpedo boats; and 7,600 marine Diesel engines. We also gave him $320 million in machine tools; $35 million in metal-cutting tools; $43 million in petroleum-refining equipment; $171 million in electric generators; 810,000 tons of non-ferrous metals; 17,600 tons of ferro-alloys; 2,688,000 tons of steel; railroads, complete factories, ships, food and billions in cash.

A CONTINUOUS WAR

For convenience in dating we speak of a "First," a "Second," and a possible "Third" World War. Actually one feels compelled to regard these as swelling crises in a continuous war. At least after the outbreak of World War Two, there would be no cessation. The "night illuminated by an unknown light" — the signal the Mother of God said would mark the beginning of the "chastisement of the world for its many transgressions" occurred on the night of January 24-25, 1938.[1]

Shortly thereafter, on March 11, Hitler entered Austria to begin a series of invasions that eventually brought all of Europe (except Portugal and Ireland) into the conflict. By the attack on Pearl Harbor Japan threw down the gauntlet to the United States on December 7 (Dec. 8, Pacific date), 1941. Today after twenty-seven years we have not yet found the formula for peace. Hundreds of thousands of American soldiers are deployed in Europe and Asia, bolstering our NATO and SEATO obligations, and other thousands are in actual combat in Vietnam. Revolutionary uprisings in the Congo, Indonesia, Rhodesia, Cuba, Santo Domingo, Panama, Suez, Algeria, Morocco, and more recently in South America, have kept the guns loaded and the camps training armies for another phase of the war, — the Third World War.

Read what Senator Styles Bridges of New Hampshire said in 1952:

"The Third World War is not in the future. We are in it now. We were in it even before the Second World War ended. Once our ground forces were joined on the Asiatic mainland with those of the enemy, it became unlikely that WE COULD EVER, short of the collapse of world Communist power, FIND PEACE AND GO HOME."

---

[1] What news reports called "an extraordinary display" of the Northern lights over Europe and America, seen as far south as the Mediterranean and Florida, Sister Lucia dos Dolores explained as a supernatural phenomenon. She explained to Father Jongen, S.V.D., what many observers noted, that unlike the Aurora Borealis, the streaks of light and color (mostly blood red) on January 24 did not originate below the horizon and shine upward, but originated at the zenith of the sky and shone downward. They were as brilliant in the southern sky as in the northern.

WHAT IS TO COME? *

We do not prophesy. We state facts and draw logical conclusions. The world revolution is now the great danger of the West and of the whole world. We do not know whether it will cross the boundaries of our country or whether the revolutionary elements in our cities will succeed, though there are signs that they may. One thing we know, that we have no more important task than to prepare for the deluge, not only militarily but spiritually. Nothing could be more fateful than to imitate the tactics of the contemporaries of Noe: to wait for the coming events eating, drinking and dancing.

Perhaps at no other time has man had a deeper understanding of the gospel of the Last Judgment. Whatever the false prophets have said of the "eternal" kingdom they built yesterday, all modern nations for years have had an uncanny presentiment of that which must come. They were afraid.

Armed millions everywhere are ready to defend so-called order and freedom and yet all tremble in fear. Capitalism has piled up gigantic sums of money. Technical science believes that nothing is impossible to man and yet he is afraid.

The apocalyptic character of the times lies in the decisive battle between the anti-God, anti-Christ and anti-Church, — in brief all the demoniacal powers of the world on one side and the divine, the Christian and Catholic on the other. But when the demoniacal reveals itself apocalyptically, ruthlessly, and world-conqueringly, then it always shows itself for what it really is, always was and always will be: pride, hatred, lies. The world-shaking apocalyptic struggle, in the midst of which we stand, is the decisive battle between truth and error.

We see the deepest theme of present day world happenings is primarily a battle between God and idols. "The problems are fundamentally theological," said General MacArthur. It has been so for five hundred years.

---

*There have been several excellent articles by "A Monsignor" in the *Christian Family Magazine* published by the Divine Word Missionary Fathers of Techny, Illinois. These articles describe the time in which we live. The above article appeared in the March, 1952, issue under the title "Behumbled Man". This priest has a world viewpoint, as his brother priests are scattered all over the earth in the Divine Word Missions.

We do not sufficiently consider a peculiarity of great world historical events. They come like earthquakes, like volcanic eruptions. They rush down from the mountains like avalanches. They are irresistible like the deluge. Man faces such things in helpless impotence. These catastrophes break all dikes.

The catastrophes of history, including world war and world revolution, are not mere accidents. They are part and parcel of a grandiose plan of divine Providence. When such a catastrophe comes we know that GREAT THINGS are in the making.

God creates from nothing. Ever and anon in the course of history we find God creating something out of nothing. Thus the Christian world was born out of the confusion of the migration of nations, out of the abyss of perverse paganism and unbelieving Judaism.

So it is today. Today we face — of course, only in a certain sense, for Christianity lives on amongst us, and cannot be wholly destroyed — A NEW NOTHING, A NEW CHAOS. The world seems to have squandered the last remnants of Christian culture. IT IS PAGANIZED TO THE CORE. The glorious heritage of the early Church and the Middle Ages is consumed, not by the Church but by the world. That was the great theological task of total wars and their aftermath, the world revolution, to prove irrefutably that we have reached a point in which dark chaos stares us in the face. That is the time which had to come to create a new world. God creates this new world out of nothing, just as He did at the beginning of time, at the deluge, at the collapse of the Roman Empire.

Communism is a power of immense Satanic and destructive force. Its appearance is usually combined with the failure of political authority. Consequently the individual and his rights are defenseless and helpless. There is no law to protect him and even almighty capital is powerless in such times. Communistic tyranny is anti-God and anti-human, but like the world wars, it has a God-intended mission. And the mission is to HUMBLE MODERN PRIDE.

Modern pride was born when humanism was born. Humanism placed man in the center of all things, made man the measure of all things. Protestantism continued this deification process by the doctrine of private interpretation of the Scriptures and liberalism completed it by its unbounded mania for freedom in every realm of human endeavor. It took five hundred years to complete this man-idolizing process. On the eve of the first world war this Babylonian dream reached the limit set by God. Modern man believed himself to be everything, to know everything, to be able to do everything and above all to be his own master. He had become a god.

Communism proves that man does not know all, cannot do all, cannot have all, in other words that he is not God. It makes man small and poor and humble.

When God creates new worlds He begins with nothing. Man must learn to do like God. He must learn that he is nothing before God; he must become humble. If and when the communists come we all must become small again, bow our heads before the great eternal God, before His word and His law. With that will come the conversion of all.

THINK!

—Satan, look at the fools,
  Fighting, tearing each other apart for they know not
      why
  You gave them hate,
—Yes . . . but . . .

—Look at them, haughty, arrogant
  Believing themselves great, clever, upright
  You gave them pride,
  Are you not satisfied?
—Yes . . . but . . .

—Look at them amassing fortunes
  Look at them, despoiling, exploiting one another
  You gave them greed,
  Are you not satisfied?
—Yes . . . but . . .

—They burn up with envy
  Lust, gluttony abases them
  Anger drives them crazy;
  Laziness sweeps away shame
  Do they not well accomplish
  All you want them to do?
—Yes . . . but . . .

—Satan, you are the great Conqueror!
—No, I am, as always, the great Conquered.
—Who, then, is the Conqueror, Satan?
—*Love.*

Emanuel Barhey (Les Chants de la Vie)
Editions de la Revue Internationale (Bruxelles).

Part 2

Political Dangers

Chapter 2

The Cause Is Atheism

By DEAN CLARENCE MANION *
The Keynote Speech at *The Wanderer* Forum, 1965

In 1950 I published the *Key To Peace*. Tonight, some years later, what I am really proposing is a declaration of war.

What I am going to make into the predicate of this discourse, is pretty awful. I know before I start that this predicate is going to be very hard for you or for any human being to promptly comprehend.

I don't expect you to fully comprehend what I am going to say, because it's a little too terrible.

I say deliberately and after careful consideration that our American civilization is sick, seriously sick, and the illness is probably terminal. The chances are ten to one that this magnificent civilization which goes by the name of our American way of life is on the way out . . . for good.

The fact is, my friends, that our American civilization, as the symbol of Western civilization, is seriously sick. There are three symptoms which are all that I propose to talk about, which prove conclusively in my estimation, that there is a malignancy under this civilization which is eating out its heart. One of these symptoms is the prevalence of major crimes. The second symptom is Communism and the third symptom is the all but complete collapse of the American constitutional system.

Now I have expatiated and so have you, innumerable times about each one of these three symptoms as though it was the disease itself. Crime and cure of crime and the cause of crime; Communism and the dastardly, evil, diabolical nature of Communism, how many times have all of us gone after that as though here is the great disease that afflicts civilization and threatens

---
*Permission to print given by Wanderer Printing Co., St. Paul, Minnesota

THE HONORABLE
DEAN CLARENCE MANION

to wipe out mankind. And the collapse of the American constitutional system, — who has not stood up or heard other people stand up and speak about the Supreme Court of the United States, and about a callous Congress that wipes out constitutional limitations, about the defiance of the will of the Founding Fathers and the foreboding indications of this collapse of constitutional limitations and the Bill of Rights.

Now the fact is, — and tonight we can disclose it and tell the truth, — the fact is that crime is not a disease in itself, nor is Communism, nor is the collapse of the American constitutional system.

THE CAUSE OF THESE THINGS IS THE UNDERLYING CANCER OF ATHEISM WHICH IS EATING OUT THE HEART OF OUR CIVILIZATION.

The sooner, my friends, that we realize this, that we see that crime is not a cause, it's a result of a cause; that Communism is not a disease, it is the symptom of a more serious disease; and that the collapse of our constitutional system is not something that comes about because of the ineptitude of the Supreme Court or the callousness of a Congressman or the apathetic indifference of the American people. The collapse of our constitutional system along with these other two symptoms is a result of this deeper malignancy that moves our civilization to the grave. And unless we recognize the seat of this disturbance, unless we quit treating symptoms as ends and objects of treatment in themselves, unless we quit scratching the surface and dig deeper, then this death is going to be hastened.

Now let us take crime as a symptom of the atheistic malignancy. How come? Well, all of us have heard innumerable people talk about crime and the cause of crime, the magnification of crime and so on and so forth.

How many people who talk about crime stop to point out that every major crime is a sin against God before it is an offense against the State. Have YOU ever heard that? How many people who tell you that we need more policemen and larger Federal appropriations and more astute and vigorous courts have ever paused to point out the immorality of this act in the first place?

One man has. A man who knows more about crime than anybody in the United States: J. Edgar Hoover. Let me read you something he has said. "The moment has arrived" — this was at Loyola University last November — "the moment has arrived when we must face realistically the startling fact that since 1958 crime in this Country has increased five times faster than the population. Serious crimes, murder, forcible rape, burglary, aggravated assault, automobile theft have mounted steadily since the end of World War II. In 1951 these crimes for the first time topped the one-million mark and more than two and a quarter million serious crimes were reported during '63 and more than that were totaled up during '64. Even more ominous is the fact that this came about through a growing wave of youthful criminality across the Nation. Last year for the fifteenth consecutive year, crimes involving our young people increased over the previous year. "For all serious crimes committed in the United States," — now mind you, get this — "for all serious crimes reported in '63, seventy-two percent of total arrests for those crimes were children under twenty years of age. What a grim, unhappy commentary," he says, "on the moral climate of this nation. The moral strength of our Nation has decreased alarmingly. This breakdown in our moral standards can only render us impotent as a people and as a Nation."

What remedy does this great man propose for all of this? More Federal appropriations, more detection devices perhaps and more astute and realistic court judgments? These would all help. Nobody deprecates the importance of this or any other remedy for these crimes. But Mr. Hoover recommends . . . none of these things.

"We must return to the teachings of God if we are to cure this sickness. As Americans we must learn to trust God, to know God, to know His teachings and to live His ways."

This is a large order. But this is a fact.

Crime is a sin and the reason why crime is increasing at this astounding rate in proportion to our population is that more people are sinning and fewer people are imbued with a love and faith and fear of God. That's the trouble.

How many sermons have we heard talking about crime and the cure of crime in terms of the moral laws? Not many!

Atheism, the indifference to God, the secularization of our criminal concepts and criminal remedies, this is reflected in the statistics that Mr. Hoover is forced to report month after month and year after year. Crime is symptom number one of the growing indifference on the part of our population to God and to the laws of God and to the Commandments of God. Crime isn't going to get any better no matter how many more policemen you add until we do something about this basic cause.

Last Sunday on the Manion Forum my daughter interviewed Chief William H. Parker of the City of Los Angeles. She asked him this very direct question when he told about the difficulties of enforcing the law; when he told about the impediments of court judgments and the sympathetic mamby-pamby type of softhead that comes in pleading for the criminal and criticizing the cop. She said: "Do you think that revival of religion would help any in solving this crime problem, Chief?" "Oh," he said, "of course it would; it would not only help, but, if it were carried to its logical conclusion, it would cure it. But," he said: "Miss Manion, I'm sorry to say and I want to repeat this" — and he did repeat it in the course of this broadcast — : "Our Country today is more than half pagan."

We are supposed to be a Christian nation, if you please. But this man is up against the truth of reality. He knows the kind of people who are violating the laws and the kind of people who are propagating this violation. If you could just have a heart-to-heart talk with the average police chief in the average city, he could tell you so very many things that he can't get published, that he wouldn't dare announce about people and about movements and about immorality and about atheism and about Communism, of course. Chief Parker is no exception to that rule.

The second symptom: Communism!

Communism is not just atheism, it is anti-theism! Communism is anti-God! It is the activated atheism which, for the first time in human history, has ridden successfully across a third of the world and keeps on going in spite of all of our protestations, in spite of all of our foreign aid and in spite of all the deafness and blindness with which we insist upon regarding it.

I have some more documentation. I don't want you to take my word for it.

Here's what Whittaker Chambers says about Communism. This is in one of the most remarkable books ever written, called *The Witness*. It should be *must* reading for people like us. We should pore over it because this man is emptying his soul of all of its experiences in his excursion into Communism and back again. Whittaker Chambers says that Communism is what happens — now get this — not when somebody gets hungry and feels underprivileged or notices his lack of education or is pushed around in his neighborhood or by the cops or any of these things.

Whittaker Chambers says: "Communism is what happens when the mind of man divorces itself from God." It is just as simple as that.

Now can we all please remember that? That when the mind of

man "divorces itself from God" Communism takes place, Communism happens! Communism happens, in other words, to the intellectual, not to the harum-scarum fellow who may join up and carry a banner, but who never thinks. Communism is a part of a thought process. A mind is emptied of its conception of God and the heart is emptied of its faith in God and Communism moves into the vacuum. Because the man who ceases to worship God must immediately start to worship something. That is in his nature which he cannot deny or disintegrate because the Author of nature continues to be above and beyond his boasts in spite of himself.

Chambers goes on and says that "The Communist crisis consequently results from our indifference to God." One doesn't have to be a militant atheist, one may be an agnostic. God makes no difference to him. He is simply consumed with secularism and secular remedies.

Ladies and Gentlemen, if God made the world and everybody in it, how can you move Him out of any consideration in its management? And yet, that's what we have done. Indifference to God. It isn't atheism so much as it is Godlessness in our procedures and in our prescriptions that is at the root of this Communistic development because indifference first, agnosticism and then atheism and then, of course, you move inevitably into the Communist orbit because you have no place else to go.

Faith, says Chambers, is the central problem of our civilization. Faith in God or faith in man. Of course, the Communists come forth with this boundless faith in the perfectability of human nature under the iron rule of the Communist lash. But what propels this, what gives this poise and purpose and direction is atheism. You can't counteract it in any other way except by belief.

Let's get on to a little stronger stuff. Here's Bishop Sheen.

Indifference merely? Ah, Bishop Sheen says: "Communism is not satisfied with mere denial of God. It demands defiance of God." Under Marxism he said that "titanism of denial has become the titanism of defiance, and defiance becomes" — get this — "demonic when it imposes its own will upon the world or else proclaims its own divinity."

So let's face it, my friends, this is not just indifference. This is not just atheism. This is anti-theism! The author of anti-theism is the Devil. Communism is hell-born and hell-bent, and, if you can't see THAT, you can never fight it adequately!

Many of my sophisticated friends, good people, religious people, tell me over and over again, that Communism is a by-product of poverty and it will go away quietly, whenever there are enough things, material things, to go around all over the world. And, of course, that is their aim and that is their object and that is the procedure of people who direct the policies of our Government and the other governments of the world, now supposed to be anti-Communist. Just keep everyone well fed and Communism will quietly disappear when the body is no longer hungry or uncomfortable. Of course, if the things don't multiply rapidly enough to be equated with the people — well, of course, we'll just kill a few people, stop the increase in population and do away with the old who are no longer productive so that we will match up the things with the people ... one way or the other, you see.[1]

Population explosion! What do we do about it? Oh, we're going to have to do something about it, you see, because population keeps exploding. In India, for instance, the infant mortality rate keeps going down. And, since we never give them enough foreign aid, we have to do something about the babies. Next, we'll have to do something about the old people.

Why should we do this? Well, why not, for goodness' sake? We are so obsessed with this passion for pure materialism that materialistic remedies run out of the mouth of a person even when he pauses in his prayers.

This is exasperating! I have no great problem in debating Linus Pauling who shouted with every other sentence: "I am Godless." Thank God for that. I'd hate to think he was in my corner. And Eric Fromm, who likes to hear you pronounce his name like Freud. These people are Godless. They admit it and they are proceeding to make over the world with whatever faith they have, which is faith in man. They'll sneak into a conference

---

[1] "You must strive to multiply bread so that it suffices for the tables of mankind, and not rather favor an artificial control of birth, which would be irrational, in order to diminish the number of guests at the banquet of life." — Pope Paul VI, Oct. 4, 1965, U.N.

on *Pacem in Terris* and use the Pope's name under false pretenses if they can do it. That's just fine. After all, the end justifies the means in such a case, because you have no conscience, you have no moral law. I'm reminded of what David Lawrence reported after Alexei Adzubai had his famous press conference with Pope John. He was the only newspaperman the Pope saw privately and all other newspapermen wanted to know what the Pope told him. So they jumped to the conclusion that the Pope was about ready to make some sort of concordat with the Kremlin. When Alexei came out smiling from ear to ear — he was Khrushchev's son-in-law, remember, the principal mouthpiece of the Communist movement in those days, editor of *Pravda* or *Izvestia*, or both —, they said: "Alexei, is the Pope going to make an agreement with the Kremlin?" With disarming frankness, Alexei said: "Of course not. The Pope knows that I am an atheist and that Communism is atheism. As an atheist, I wouldn't have to keep an agreement that I made with the Pope, and Pope John knows that." This from Alexei Adzubai!

But how many Americans don't know it. How many people who have made the more than one thousand agreements with the Communists, multilateral and bilateral, didn't know as much as Alexei candidly admitted there in Rome that day. The Pope knows, and everybody should know that, as an atheist, he (Alexei) wouldn't have to keep any agreement. He could break it. An atheist can't make a binding agreement. Anybody who can make a binding agreement or who is bound by it in moral law should avoid agreements with atheists. That he didn't say, but you would go on to say it.

Yet, we've made thousands of agreements with them. We pretend to co-exist with them. And here is the basis of this whole situation, atheism, which rules out any possibility of doing any kind of business with these people because they are not dependable by the standards of morality which is the basis of our civilization. Activated atheism! Faithlessness on horseback! Not just agnosticism, not just indifference to God.

When Americans lose their convictions they lose their reason for the continuity of their civilization. When I see evidences of the fact that conviction is gone . . . When I stood before an audience bigger than this at the University of Wisconsin and

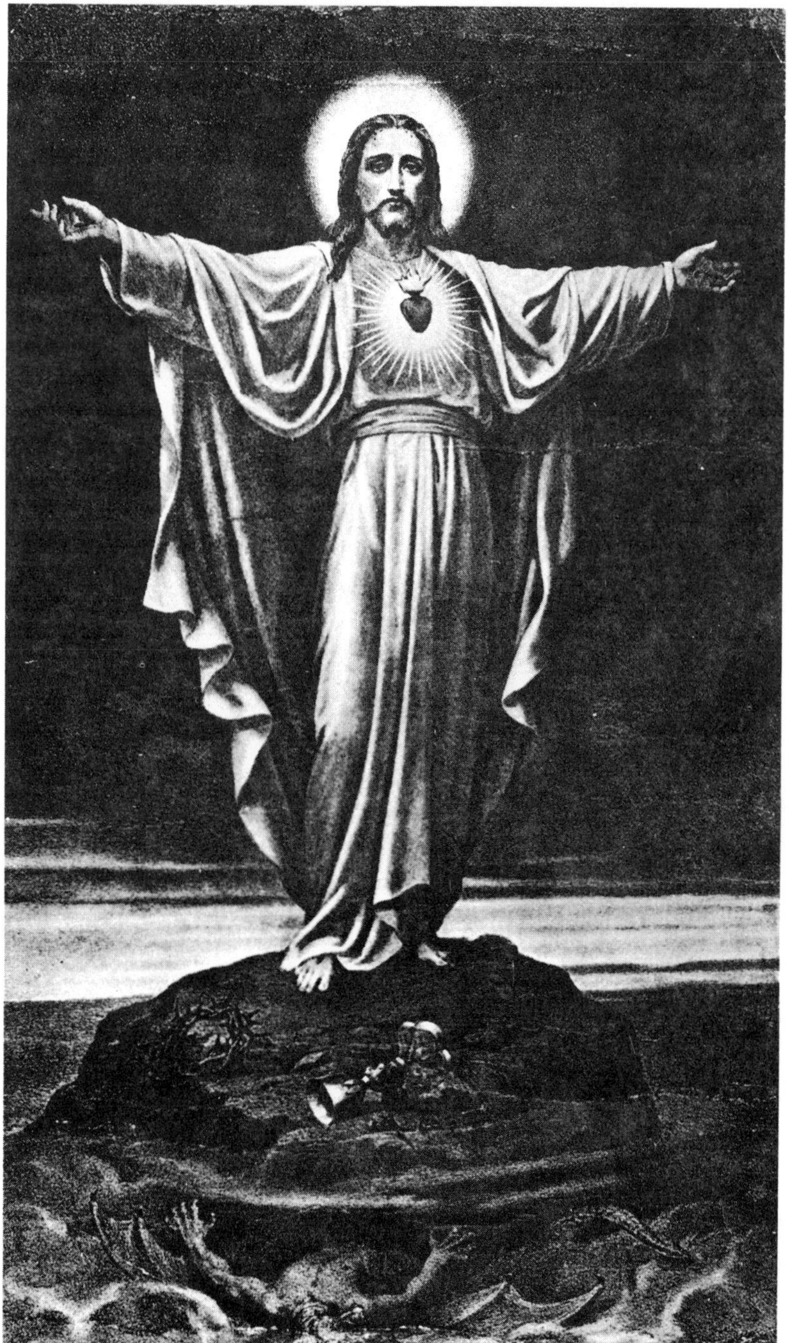

repeated the Declaration of Independence — words that are so solemn and so stirring that it's difficult for me to pronounce them without emotion —: "All men are created," — do you know what that provoked at the University of Wisconsin? The wildest, most hysterical laughter that I have ever heard in my life! A group of two hundred fifty members of the Socialist club who had filled all the front seats roared with laughter every time I mentioned God or the Constitution or the Declaration of Independence!

This was a frightening experience. To see what our taxes are supporting under the name of education!

Indifference to God? What does it produce? I put out a broadcast on it a few weeks ago which was inspired by the articles in the *Saturday Evening Post*. Did you see those beautiful boys and girls stretched across the sidewalk with their arms around each other sitting in and lying in, the filthy speech movements, and so on and so forth? What sort of exploitation is made of these things in enemy countries! This is a terribly shocking fruit to pick after all of the labors that we have spent in planting the tree.

But then I have more demoralizing evidence than that. Here is something that I am reluctant even to read. Here is something that was said by a very prominent Catholic educator, a priest, a scholarly man, addressing a group of representatives of independent, non-tax-supported schools. Why is the independent school? What is it for? What should it teach? Why would it continue to exist?

I have attended those conventions. I know something about what these people feel, Protestant and Catholic and independent. They all have a very, very good thesis upon which to continue their independent education. Very vital to the continuity of freedom. But, unfortunately, that isn't what this man said. I combed this speech carefully, line by line, to find some reference you might expect from a Catholic educator talking to a convention of independent school superintendents who had made him their chief guest. Well, here are some of the things: "The three things I would like to talk about here," he said, "are human emancipation, which is a very interesting process in our day." Get that . . . emancipation. "Human developments and lastly technological innovation. All of these processes — human emancipation, human developments and technological innovation

— are interrelated and interlocked. First then, the process of human emancipation. To me, it has been a startling fact that more nations have become independent political entities since the close of World War II than the total of existing nations prior to the war. About a billion people, a third of mankind have passed from colonial to free status since the war."

Ladies and Gentlemen, when you speak of a billion people since World War II, what comes into your mind? Liberation? Emancipation? . . . or Slavery? This man was talking about the Congo and Ghana and Chad, I suppose. A billion of the people have escaped from the "slavery of colonialism" which was Western civilization, if you please. And this is something to cheer about. Where is another billion? Not people emancipated from the jungle, but people who were robbed of a thousand years of Christian heritage. What about the billion people in Catholic Poland and Catholic Hungary, Romania, Latvia, Lithuania and the Ukraine? Is this the age of emancipation — God help us! — or is this the age of progressive slavery?

Not a word about God. Not a word about Communism. All about emancipation, technological development and change!

Now I wouldn't attribute bad faith to anybody. Certainly not to this person. I have the greatest respect for his intellect and his good will. But, Ladies and Gentlemen, a man who can look an audience in the face and talk about the emancipation of a billion people since World War II has a more widely developed blind spot than any man should have in charge of any educational institution in this Country that I know of.

Just one more citation, if you can stand it. He tells about the small school and its contribution to the progress of the world. There have been many such and there still are — God bless them! He says: "I like to think of one small school in Hungary that turned out three very famous men — Edward Teller, the father of the H-Bomb; Leo Zellard, a famous physicist with Einstein; and John Von Neuman, the father of the computer." That's all about Hungary, if you please. What about Cardinal Mindszenty? What about the institutions in Hungary where they don't turn people OUT any more; they turn people IN and lock the door? Where is this school today, that's what I want to know, and how free is it and whom is it turning out and whom is it locking in?

How can you possibly fight Communism when the leaders of our intellectual communities, so-called, are so completely blind and deaf and dumb to the realities of slavery? This is a terrible reflection upon our generation and upon our faith. Communism is increasing in respectability in the estimation of the intellectual community and even in the estimation of the religious community, by and large.

Our churches for the most part, let's face it, are now substituting a social consciousness for the individual personal conscience. Church leaders seem to think that, if you just give them enough laws, they can make a good society out of bad men. It won't be necessary to reform the individuals; all you have to do is just get after the legislatures and forget the Ten Commandments, forget the reformation of the human soul and think collectively. Be socially conscious, improve Society, and to hell with the people in it.

We have developed a passion for civil rights. A civil right is something that comes from the civil government. The Declaration of Independence didn't talk about civil rights. It talked about God-given rights and God-given responsibilities. But our passionate pursuit of civil rights — with no reflection upon that objective and no reflection upon the pursuit and no reflection upon the reform that the pursuit entails — let it simply be said that our passionate pursuit of civil rights in this Country has not been adequately compensated by adequate insistence upon the necessity for increased personal, moral responsibility. So far have we gone in that respect that an illegal means is now the proper approach to the establishment of a so-called civil right.

Finally, the third symptom, the collapse of constitutional government. Atheism, my friends, is being reflected in the relaxation and the degeneration of our constitutional limitations upon government, and atheism is entirely responsible for the collapse of constitutional government in this Country. I say to you, as one who has spent a quarter of a century or more now in close study and teaching of constitutional law: if there is no God, then constitutional government doesn't make sense. And that is precisely why the Founding Fathers began the organization of our political society in 1776 with an invocation of God's blessing and a profound certification of His power and His providence, to say nothing of His existence. And that is why, as the toastmaster said, forty-nine of fifty State constitutions in this Country begin as yours begins: We the people of the State of Minnesota, We the people of the State of Illinois, *grateful to Almighty God for these liberties,* do ordain and establish this Constitution for the State of Illinois and Indiana and Florida and New York and so on.

Now, there weren't any illusions about it; if there wasn't a God, there wouldn't be any God but government, and if government was God, it would be sacrilege to try to limit it with a bill of rights. Who tells God what to do? Nobody tells the Soviet Government what to do. The Soviet Government is SUPREME! Because in its lexicon there is no God but the State. And while God is revered and is in His heaven, and while the faithful of any country know that and act accordingly, then constitutional restrictions are in order; because, as William Penn said many years ago: "Those people who will not be governed by Almighty God must be ruled by tyrants." And the converse of that proposition is true, too. Never forget it. If you don't want to be ruled by tyrants, you had better acknowledge the governance of God Almighty.

And then you go back for the moral rationalization of our constitutional system — and where do you find it? In the words of Jesus Christ: "Render therefore unto Caesar only those things which are Caesar's and to God the things that are God's," and the Constitution of the United States and the constitution of every one of the constituent States renders unto Caesar what it is necessary for Caesar to have in order to preserve order and avoid anarchy, and the rest is reserved to the governance of God; to the individual's personal conscience. We have verification of that from the Father of the Constitution himself, James Madison. In *Federalist* thirty-nine you are told. (Madison was writing these *Federalist Papers* to try to get the Constitution of the United States adopted after it had been proposed by the Philadelphia Convention. And his friends told him: "This Constitution won't work, James; you've tied down the Government, you've barb-wire entangled it; it has no power. This Government is an insult to the very idea of government as we've understood it. It has no power, it won't work, it won't last, and why should we adopt it?" And Madison answered classically; he said: "We have staked the whole future of our American civilization, not upon the power of government. Far from it! We have staked the whole future of our American civilization upon the capacity of our citizens to govern themselves." To govern themselves, to restrain themselves, to demean themselves under the Ten Commandments of God.)

My friends, as long as the people of this Country can so demean themselves, as long as they acknowledge the existence of their Creator and obey His Commandments, as long as they have a passionate devotion not merely to civil rights but to personal moral responsibility, then we can restore and maintain the Constitutional limitations upon our Government. Only people who are so inspired by faith in God and obedience to His commands can afford the great luxury of keeping Caesar in his place, and Christ said as much, because when the people are not governed by God a tyrant will move into the vacuum as Penn said it would and as it is doing now.

Do you know what the constitutional law of this Country is? It's the last Executive order of the President of the United States. Whatever he says in the next twenty-four hours, you must do! He probably won't say it because he is a moral man. Unlike Castro, or Chou En-lai, or some of these characters who have gone the distance over the Communist chasm. No, moral restraints, fortunately, have restrained our public officers for the most part. He doesn't order people stood against the wall and shot, as Castro does, because he knows that is immoral.

Just remember this, please, that governments and governors have two forms of restrictions placed upon them. One is legal: that you find in the Constitution; the other is moral, which you find in the Ten Commandments. Fortunately, our leaders today have been men of basic morality. You are being protected against autocracy now, not by what the Constitution of the United States says, but by the moral instincts of the people who hold the reins of government in this Country.

But, when some of these people in our intellectual community who deny God, when people like Linus Pauling and Eric Fromm get to be President, what is going to restrain them from ordering people to the wall as Castro does? The Constitution is gone, moral restraints are gone, and the people live in terror. So, when you see constitutional limitations collapsing, you see reflected in this ruin of this magnificently conceived institution, you see reflected there the radiations from this malignancy which is eating the heart out of the American way of life.

So let's start treating not the symptoms, if you please, but the crime, the Communism, the collapse of our constitutional system. Let's not blame it all on the Supreme Court or all upon the Congressmen or all upon the apathetic indifference of the American people who won't write their Congressmen and tell them to beat this or beat that. Let's get down to basics. Let's put our finger on the cause of this consequence. In the words of Brigham Young: "Let us tell the truth and divide the people."

* * *

GOD IS DEAD PSYCHOSIS[1]

Increasingly we hear among "advanced" Protestant clergymen the Nietzchean refrain, "God is dead," by which it is meant that we should concern ourselves with this world and its problems and forget about anything beyond.

Daily we find evidence that God is dead as far as the conscious belief of many is concerned. God "died" in Supreme Court thinking at least as late as 1962, when the Schempp decision regarded the mention of His name in national documents as evidence only of the authors' personal belief. Only recently the Court denied a hearing to New York City parents who sought an order allowing their children to "pray voluntarily to God each day" in a Queens public school.

Only a few days ago the interment in Canterbury Cathedral of Somerset Maugham, a writer who believed in neither God nor the after-life, accentuated the paradox of a Christianity without faith.

The God-is-dead psychosis shows itself in some macabre ways. Recently the Life Extension Society took out an ad in a national magazine urging prospective members to consider being frozen at death, their bodies to be kept in cold storage until such time as science brings them back to life in youth — testimony at once of a desire for immortality and of a lack of belief in heaven.

The deep-freezing fantasy suggests one reason why "God is dead" in so many modern minds . . .

---

[1] Paul Hallett in *The Register* Dec. 26, 1965

GODLESSNESS IN GOVERNMENT

The crisis facing the world should not be based only on symptoms that appear in one country. Russia is indeed the super-culprit, for from Russia have come the political errors that have beset the world for nearly fifty years. We must remember the plan devised by the Bolsheviks back in 1911 — to conquer the world. The godless philosophy by which they would attain their goal has oozed out from beneath the Iron Curtain and has permeated governments everywhere. Some have withstood the evil better than others. Some will stand up against the tide longer than others, but we would do ourselves an injustice were we to ignore its effect in our own country.

The deadly philosophy of Liberalism, falsely honored by the name of Rationalism, got its start in the days of the French Revolution. In 1793 the enthronement of Reason was enacted in the Cathedral of Notre Dame in Paris, when an actress was placed on the High altar as the Goddess of Reason. The revolt against God was underway.

This revolt has since been known as the Deification of Man after the writings of Rousseau and Voltaire. A progressive effort was started to overthrow Christianity, to destroy Christ's Church and to set aside the Christian order which He had established. The Church was made a department of State, whose office was the promotion of moral order. "In the life of the Church the emperor shall be supreme, and now in one edict after another, the bishops were forbidden to receive or take account of papal decrees without the emperor's consent, forbidden to communicate with Rome, even to ask faculties from Rome, and forbidden to issue pastoral letters until the imperial censor had approved them. 'Useless' monasteries and convents (i.e., those of contemplative orders) were suppressed, 318 in all out of a total number of 915. . . State examinations were to determine clerical promotions, and in place of the various diocesan seminaries and the houses of study of the monastic orders, the emperor founded twelve new State seminaries, in which alone the clergy, secular and regular, were to be trained. The directors and staffs of these seminaries were carefully chosen from the Liberals among the clergy — not a few of them were Freemasons —

and a current of liberal thought was thereby introduced into Austrian ecclesiastical life which continued to be a force until well on into the nineteenth century . . . The number of candles to be lit on the altar for Mass, the prayers to be used, the hymns to be sung were carefully fixed by imperial decree. There was to be but one Mass daily, and this must be said at the High Altar — all other altars were to be removed. . . The breviary was carefully censored and such feasts as that of St. Gregory VII were forbidden. Sermons on Christian doctrine were not allowed, the Litany of Loreto was forbidden, and the Rosary too. The monstrance was not to be used for exposition of the Blessed Sacrament." (Hughes, Philip, *A Popular History of the Catholic Church*, 217-218.)

These throttling limitations spread wherever Christianity had gained a foothold. These theorists became sufficiently influential to bring on wars to accomplish any end. The real leaders of these activities have always remained underground. This worldwide menace has been directed in secret by God-haters who prospered under Christian umbrellas, which they sought to destroy. The extent of the underground movement, and the allied forces behind it, has never been measured. It has always remained a secret society which has had as its reason for existence, the de-Christianizing of society.

Without some knowledge of this underground movement no one is able to comprehend true causes behind present-day events and their relation to wars. Back of long-range planning is the determination to bring forth a new materialistic age involving inevitably the complete disappearance of what we have understood as Christian civilization.

That a movement to suppress the Church — and all religion — has been underway in a secret fashion has been written about by Denis Fahey in *The Kingship of Christ*, and in a most interesting way by Julian Sterne in a volume called *The Secret of the Zodiac*.[1] Sterne is a world student of Secret Societies, and under the guise of a novel he has written what he explains is not fiction but sober fact; that a world figure, functioning through secret agents known only to him — not even to one another — is the hidden force that manipulates the armies of the world,

---

[1] Sterne, Julian, *The Secret of the Zodiac*, London, Boswell, 1934.

pitting them against one another while arranging for them sometimes actually to furnish each other the firearms and ammunition with which to fight. (It is reported that England, for instance, was actually selling weapons to Germany during the First World War, in which these two countries were at war with each other, and that the U.S. was selling scrap iron to Japan right up to the hostilities that brought our nations into opposite camps.) Is it possible that such a secret organization, headed by Satan himself, is directing the events of our century, which are leading us ever closer to the cataclysm and denouement predicted by so many mystics and by Holy Scripture itself?

At the International Congress held in Paris in 1889 to celebrate the centenary of the French Revolution, one of the orators of the occasion, Brother Louis Amiable, declared that the reorganization of the Grand Orient in 1773 was the distant preparation and fore-runner of the great Revolution of 1789. "The regime," said he, "inaugurated by the Grand Orient gave force and vigour. to that great truth which was to be formulated sixteen years later by the declaration of the rights of man and the citizen: 'The law is the expression of the general will'."

Compare what another author, Francolin, said on the same occasion:

> The day will come when monarchies and religions will collapse. That day is not far off and we are awaiting it. . . That day will bring about the masonic universal fraternity of peoples, the ideal which we have set for ourselves. It is our business to hasten its coming.

"Permit me to give expression to my hope that Freemasonry, which has done so much for the emancipation of mankind, and to which history is indebted for national revolutions, will succeed in bringing about that still greater revolution — the International Revolution." (Official Bulletin of Grand Loge de France, October, 1922).

"We brought about the French Revolution; our ancestors thought it was to set them free. No such thing; it was simply a change of masters. . . Yes, we guillotined the King. Long live the State-King! We dethroned the Pope. Long live the State-Pope! We are driving out God, as the gentlemen of the right express it. Long live the State-God." (Thus sneered Clemenceau in the Senate, November 17, 1903. Quoted in *L'Eglise Catholique et la Droit Commun,* by l'Abbe Roul, p. 48.)

Almost any page of French history since 1870 will bear out the attempts made by the Masons to realize these subversive plans to destroy the old Christian society based on revealed and spiritual truths, and to establish a universal republic which dispenses altogether from a belief in God and a superior world. Is it possible that our beloved America has been drawn into such a plot, and if unawares, that our leaders have been hoodwinked into treacherous courses?[1] We need but quote the official publication of the Soviet government to prove that whole legions of the most cunning demons have been dispatched from hell to help the Communists destroy the Christian religion.

"The Soviet power must exert the most fervent propaganda against religion. All religions are one and the same poison, intoxicating and deadening the mind, the will, and the conscience; a fight to the death must be declared against them. Our task is not to reform, but to destroy all kinds of religion, all kinds of morality."

No wonder that Pope Pius XII called Communism Satanism. No wonder that the Catholic Church, which is the true kingdom of God on earth, suffers persecution in so many countries behind the Iron Curtain. No wonder that since Communism began to incite persecution against the Church, more millions of martyrs have given their lives for Christ than during the previous nineteen centuries.[2]

Lunacharsky, Commissar of Public education, declared at Moscow: "We hate Christians and Christianity; even the best of them must be looked upon as our worst enemies. They preach the love of neighbors and mercy which is contrary to our principles. Christian love is an obstacle to the development of our

---

[1] *The Register,* Denver, Colo., Dec. 19, 1965, page 2.

[2] Thilges, Rev. John J., *Satan Will Tempt You,* Divine Word Publications, Techny, Ill. 1959

revolution. Down with the love of our neighbors; WHAT WE WANT IS HATRED. We must learn to hate, and it is only then that we shall conquer the world." (Congressional Record, Vol. 77, pp 1539-40)

Chapter 3

Launching S.S. *Vincent Harrington*, Liberty Ship 362, July 22, 1944. Mrs. Vincent Harrington and daughter officiating.

MAJOR VINCENT HARRINGTON[1]

The mother of Major Vincent Harrington and my own mother were girlhood friends 85 years ago in the pioneer days of Iowa. Vincent and I were boyhood friends. I married his sister. He was elected to the Congress of the United States from Iowa on the Democratic ticket in 1936 and served in Congress for six years until the day after Pearl Harbor. He was very much opposed to the idea that there should ever be war, and stated on the floor of Congress that "If I ever vote to send the sons of American mothers to war in foreign lands, I will go with them. There never was a good war or a poor peace."

I was with him in Washington on Pearl Harbor Day. On this day I asked him these questions: Who is behind Roosevelt and from whom does he take orders? He replied: "Those are my questions. I have asked nearly every Congressman and Senator and many others who should know the answers to those same questions, and the replies I received have all been the same: 'I do not know.' However, the general impression has been that

---

[1] He was a young American Congressman who abhorred war. He invited no man to danger he was not ready to share. He served the land of his birth as a Christian who loved God, and in the end gave his life for his country. His body lies in a hero's grave across the Atlantic. His soul is with God among the Communion of Saints.

Roosevelt is taking instructions and following orders from internationalists, and some of them are citizens of foreign lands." The next day Vincent voted to declare war on Japan and Germany. The same day he resigned from Congress, joined the army, went to war, and gave his life for his country in Europe early in World War II.

What is said in this chapter in no way applies to any Democrats, or to anyone who, as I did, helped vote in the New Deal, or to any true American who has served the government in any office for the past 33 years. I believe that voters and most government employees were outsiders who were organized for vote-getting purposes. I believe the New Deal was ruled by an invisible unknown cabinet of Internationalists, and the visible Brain Trusters who willingly carried out the orders of this cabinet were stooges who were given wide and unlawful powers. These men it is, who start world wars. It is to this small group of Treasonists, whose treachery we in 1966 know so well, that I address these words.

We have been betrayed! Acts of treason have been committed! In Washington since 1933 there have been men in high places who want our American Way of Life to disappear. They have been endeavoring to sovietize the glorious land of our birth. I believe the true leader of these scheming super-government internationalists is none other than Satan.

I love my fellow Americans — love them as I love my native land. America has been good to my people . . . and as America is a conglomeration of all people — I love these people of all nationalities, all races, all religions, and all creeds. I love these people, because I love God, who created all of us in His own image. There is a commandment that we should have loved Joe Stalin as ourselves because — he was our neighbor. We can fight Communism and the devil best by loving God and our neighbor. We must despise Communism because it is Godless, but must pity and pray for the Communist leaders who are victims of Satan; and the same applies to all Communists in our United States. "There is neither Jew nor Greek; there is neither slave nor freeman; there is neither male nor female; for you are all one in Christ Jesus." (Gal. 3:28.)

The New Deal, often supported by Godless books and

atheistic classrooms, clubbed its way into our legislative halls, courtrooms and into many branches of our National Government; and, more recently, into some businesses and professions. This was accomplished by a swarm of students from some of our universities, many of which were founded as Christian institutions with constitutional requirements to teach Christian religion — and they did so for many decades. These institutions deteriorated, following the leadership of Godless instructors, until now they are hotbeds of anti-God propaganda. These students, and their teachers, too, were taken from the universities and given positions of responsibility in the Government of the United States.

The bureaucrats did not stay in Washington — they went international, too. By secret treaties they joined other foreign anti-God governments, all determined to spread their theories to the ends of the earth, until in 1966 God is banished from one-half of the world, and ignored for the most part in the other half. The wave of Marxist tendencies is now sweeping in on all America, threatening to smother out reason and freedom, and rob us completely of our Christian heritage. While we slept in the presence of widespread materialism, happy in our prosperous dream-world, counting and hoarding profits, these crackpots with their stupid theories, stole our Christian civilization from under our very eyes. Their scheming was so bold for American Christians that our people would not believe anything so diabolical could be possible. If one wants to know the trend of the future as they plan it, tune in with what the "Professors" are saying and teaching. Read the book: "God and Man at Yale," by Wm. F. Buckley, Jr., (Regnery, Chicago, 1951) a young Yale graduate, a veteran of World War II.

This all had its beginning when we allowed Christ's Church to be rent asunder. After 400 years, this has resulted in a conglomeration of confusion, and often bitter discord among good people who all profess to be Christians, until today we have some 266 different religions in the United States. Yet over 60 per cent of the people in California told the census taker in 1950 that they had no religion; and 47 per cent of all our people, 72,000,000 Americans, when asked "What is your religion," answered: "I have none."

Little by little Americans are becoming victims of the atheistic materialism of our age. Perjury, selfishness, treason, divorce, infidelity have entrenched themselves in our society. We hear the anguished cry of children of broken homes deprived of love and care rising to our ears on all sides. We see the pitiful sight of young boys and girls whose lives are wrecked by drugs, disease, and crime. Look around you at a world swept with confused alarm, a world from which love has fled, a world which has rid itself of the ennobling fear of God to find itself cringing in the fear of man. Look around about our whole country — where do we not see crime and corruption? All these are clear signs of rotting and decay of a society from within — and we all know it.

What we understand as Communism is not a child of Moscow, and it is not an exclusive Russian way of life. Communism sprang from secret societies reaching far back to Marx. Communism was spawned by the "Revolutionists for the Deification of Man." Spawning is the multiplication of kind in vast quantities, the species always remaining the same. Their philosophy which is contrary to natural law, supported by science and technology, which made materialism more attractive, has had an effect on mankind which leads to widespread acceptance of a movement whose ulterior motive is to completely destroy and obliterate Christian civilization. That is true Communism wherever it is found.

The one time Communist, Whittaker Chambers, corroborates this. He said of Communism in the *Saturday Evening Post:* "Other ages have had visions, but they have always been different versions of the same vision: the vision of God and man's relationship to God. The Communist vision is the vision of man without God. It is the vision of man's mind displacing God as the creative intelligence of the world. . . . It is that of materialism. The tools to turn it into reality are science and technology, exclusive of all supernatural factors. . . . If man's mind is unequal to the problem of man's progress he will sink back into savagery. There has never been a society or nation without God. But history is cluttered with the wreckage of nations that became indifferent to God, and died."

This false philosophy has spread so far that the whole world now faces a great crisis that can end only in destruction of one or both of the conflicting ways of life. These underground plotters laid plans to capture without shooting one shot, the greatest of all prizes—my native land—Christian United States of America.

The present crisis in America — the attempt of "Brain Trusters" and "Professors" to crush God out of American Life is to be a part of the final all-out battle between the forces of good and the forces of evil. These destructionists, through secret alliances with foreign destructionists, plan a world-wide conquest to consolidate all world governments into one Government to be ruled over by one supreme head. Nonsense! Instead of world conquest they will bring down the wrath of God on all mankind.

These men are unknowing stooges directed by demoniac forces who, because they gave up God, are now forced all unconsciously to turn to the devil for leadership. St. Gregory the Great, in one of his homilies refers to this unfortunate class as the "diabolical mystical body." They are the elect of Satan and the precursors of Antichrist. They have been led in America for the last 33 years by none other than Satan himself. Satan said so in Earling, Iowa in 1931. When an exorcist tried to banish him into Hell, he exclaimed: "Does he not know that I must prepare the way for Antichrist? How can he banish me into Hell?" And the devil was right, for as Sister Catherine Emmerich said, "Lucifer will be unchained for a time, 50 or 60 years before the year of Christ 2000. A certain number of demons are to be let loose earlier than Lucifer."

Chapter 4

The Great Betrayal

ROOSEVELT AND WORLD WAR II

I opposed every step in United States involvement in World War II. I said it would be the GARGANTUAN JEST of all history if we gave aid to Stalin in the war. I said the result would be to spread Communism over the whole world. That was my gospel and I have no regret. — HERBERT HOOVER

The United States did not drift into World War Two. Or if so, a terrible trap set for us was so cleverly contrived that the President and his cabinet — and perhaps much of the Congress — fell into it, and at a time when 80 per cent of the American people were opposed to entering the war, we were actually committed by a declaration of war to send American boys abroad.

If we give our President credit for sincerity, on October 30, 1940, when he told the mothers of America over the radio: "I have said this before, and I say it again and again, your boys are not going to be sent into any foreign wars," then he must have been unaware of the plotting soon to become evident to all the world to draw America into the maelstrom.

Books published by naval officers and historians indicate that Roosevelt had received advance information about the sneak attack on Pearl Harbor. These writers imply, if they do not say it, that our President knew it would take a military catastrophe to justify our entrance into the war. If these writers are correct, the Sunday morning surprise party at Pearl Harbor, if not deliberately planned by Americans, was the result of negligence by the Commander-in-Chief of the Armed Forces, which cost the lives of 2,326 American boys, destroyed eight of the nine capital ships of our Pacific fleet, and the garrisons of Guam, Wake, and Luzon. This great military tragedy brought about an immediate and all but unanimous approval of Congress for entrance into World War Two on the feast day of Our Lady's Immaculate Conception.

There are many who feel that President Roosevelt deliberately planned such a debacle, and perhaps just as many who are horrified at such a charge. They feel it would have served the same purpose to have the fleet steam out of the Harbor and meet the attacking forces as to lie dormant and thus create the sympathy that would justify war. History will eventually give us the facts. I am not one to anticipate condemnation or pass premature judgment. On January 26, 1947, *The New York Times* book review treated ten books having to do with the place that will be allotted to President Roosevelt when the prosecutors and defenders have had their say, and history hands down her decision. The reviewer, Karl Schriftgiesser, speaks of FDR as "a pragmatic, emotional, intuitional, volatile, stubborn, courageous, reasonable, and reasoning man." These descriptive adjectives he draws from books that attack, defend, apologize for, explain, denounce, vindicate, condemn, exalt, and exonerate the former President. I do not feel that I can untangle the mass of evidence for and against the man, and I am willing not to impute vicious motives to one with whom I must disagree.

Pearl Harbor: The Story of a Secret War by George Morgenstern, is one book that avoids circumlocution and ambiguity. Yet it denounces the way the reputations of Admiral Kimmel and General Short were sacrificed. It will continue to raise doubts as to whether these men were victims of their own failure at Pearl Harbor and not scapegoats for the mistakes of others higher up, including the Chief of Staff, the Secretary of the Army and the Navy, and the Commander-in-Chief.

Some of the best friends I have got are Communists.
— Franklin Delano Roosevelt

Whether our President deliberately betrayed us at Pearl Harbor may be questionable, but even his staunch defenders, I think, feel that at Yalta he certainly sold us out to Stalin; not only the United States, but the whole non-Communist world as well.

Even the televised life of Roosevelt and his role in the war, ascribing the sell-out to the President's broken health and the clever sagacity of Stalin, fails to make clear whether the broken health was really the cause or the effect of an anxious and tortured conscience.

How much international pressure was brought to bear in both these instances would be something we should all like to know, or in the following incident as related in *Our Sunday Visitor*.

"The fact is that the rulers of our country from 1933 until 1948 put the world in a precarious position when a President of the United States could speak of a moral idiot like Stalin as 'Uncle Joe' and could announce that 'There is nothing wrong with Communists. Some of the best friends I have got are Communists' — and in 1948, after the massacre of Warsaw, of the Katryn Forest, of the thousands of political refugees, in the face of Siberian slaughter camps and the monolithic Kremlin tryanny, an American President could still say, 'I like old Joe. Joe's a decent fellow!' "

"Put only Americans on guard tonight." — George Washington
Valley Forge, 1777

HUNGARY DESERTED IN CRISIS

"There are no words strong enough to describe the horror and revulsion caused by the actions of the Communists in Hungary last month. World sentiment has been aroused against them as never before. It was, however, a foregone conclusion that our country would supply free Hungary with everything short of arms and men, that the UN would likewise contribute nothing that might drive out the Russians.

"Why? Because America and all the world with her is afraid of the USSR. We could put Nasser in his place, we could restore order if need be in Nicaragua, we could even take on France and England together — but not Russia. That sinister power is as great if not greater than the United States of America! Russia has the H-bomb.

"How did the USSR become so powerful? And the H-bomb, invented and developed in the United States — how did Russia get hold of it?

"The atom bomb was stolen from under our nose with the connivance of PEOPLE HIGH IN THE ADMINISTRATION, notably Harry Hopkins, who lived in the White House as the President's most intimate friend."

* * *

The national involvement in international uprisings is not necessarily wrong or unjust, all placard-toting protesters to the contrary notwithstanding. But with the best intentions we have set up such international organizations as UN, NATO, SEATO, OAS, and with each group we have found ourselves spending our national wealth and sending our military forces into the far reaches of the earth in an effort to stem the onrush of Communism.

Just when we think we have stopped it in Korea, we encounter it in Vietnam, or Santo Domingo, or on the University campuses at home. It is a ubiquitous threat to mankind.

The fact that university professors are often the infiltrating germs plants a doubt in the minds of many as to whether Communism is really the evil some say it is, and arouses the liberal craving for demonstrations and sensationalism in the students. Why should democracy be better than the "People's Republic" for China? Or Vietnam? Or Korea? What seems to be overlooked is that the tyrannical State-god of Communism always suppresses personal liberty, and with it the freedom to be a human being, fulfilling the purpose of human beings,— knowing, loving, and serving God. He is a jealous God and demands no other god.

At Fatima in 1917 this movement was clearly pointed out when the Mother of God said: "Out of Russia (then a back-broken cripple among nations) will come errors which will spread throughout the world. Whole nations will be destroyed. . ."

This threat has been sounded by the FBI for America, and those who have been able to withstand the terrible charges of "character assassination," "smear," and "McCarthy tactics," have persistently warned of the menace through such groups as the Mindszenty Foundation and others.

"By the greater number of its opponents Communism is regarded as the mortal enemy of political and democratic liberty and is combatted on this account alone. Others, deeming themselves to have a deeper understanding of it, look on Communism as a social doctrine and a system of political economy divorced from all reference to spiritual realities but yet with a certain number of achievements to its credit.

"Communism, however, as a philosophy denies the supernatural, putting in its place a pseudo-mystical cult of 'progress' threatening the essential values of the Christian Revelation. That Communism is a system rooted in Atheism is quite unknown to the majority despite the repeated pronouncements and warnings of the Church over many years.

"Perhaps the apathy of so many Christians, in face of the Communist peril, is explained by the fact that they attach more importance to the social and political implications of Communism than to its spiritual significance. For them the Party is more important than the Party's ideology; the Party's Programme, than the Party's principles. The end is forgotten in face of the tactics employed to achieve it.

"This attitude explains perhaps the seductive influence which Communism continues to exercise over certain minds even after its reiterated condemnation by the Church. Communism in its spiritual and religious character is not well known."[1]

"The facts will speak for themselves to the unprejudiced inquirer, who in following the techniques of Communist propaganda, will understand many things which he sees every day taking place under his own eyes. He will see better the "why" and "how" of this propaganda in his own country; he will see Communism in its historical and true perspective, where it stands revealed as THE GREATEST DANGER WHICH HAS BEEN KNOWN TO CHRISTIAN CIVILIZATION IN TWO THOUSAND YEARS."[2]

The vast migrations, as hundreds of thousands in every country swallowed up by Communists fled their captors in quest of freedom constitute the vision granted the children of Fatima. One day as the children recited the Angel's prayer in the cave at Cabeco, Jacinta got up suddenly and said to Lucy: "Look, do you not see all the roads and paths and fields full of people weeping for hunger and having nothing to eat?"

Without wishing to anticipate future events, this could very well have been the millions and millions of refugees: men, women, and children, aged and infirm, wandering about without food or shelter along the roads and across the fields on the occasions of the invasions of Poland, Hungary, Romania, Czechoslovakia, Greece, China, Korea, Vietnam, Cuba, etc.[1]

What we must recognize today is that Communism is a scourge threatening to reduce the human race to a pack of slaves. It is the evil we were warned in 1917 was to visit mankind unless there were a conversion in man's spiritual attitude. The conversion did not take place and the evil is now upon us.

---

[1] Albert Galter, *The Red Book of the Persecuted Church.* Westminster, Md., The Newman Press, 1957, p. 1. "This is a documented and important study of Communism as it has throttled the Christian world in this century. Those who study the proofs and revelations set out in this work will soon realize the aim of Marxist persecution, and if, as often happens, they are told that the struggle is not so fierce and that its purpose is not to combat religion, but only to strike at 'outbreaks of fanaticism' or to repress 'political resistance,' it will be enough for them to recall the undeniable facts presented in *The Red Book.*"
[2] *The Catholic Times,* London.

COMMUNISM IN SPAIN[2]

The Constitution of the Republic, reestablished in Spain on 14th April, 1931, proclaimed the principle of freedom of conscience in its article 27, guaranteeing the right to profess and practice freely any religion whatsoever; but the Republican government, far from fulfilling this promise, allowed mobs, instigated by secret powers, to celebrate the change of regime by attacking the Catholic religion. The first cases of aggression were against the convents and began on 11th May, 1931, when the Convento de las Maravillas, the Convento de las Mercedes, the Convent of the Carmelite Fathers in the Square de Espana, and that of the Sacred Hearts, in Tutor Street, were amongst those assaulted in Madrid, not to speak of others in the provinces.

In January 1931, the Government of the Republic under powers given by Article 26 of the Constitution, which authorized the suppression of any religious orders which might constitute a danger to the security of the State, suppressed the Order of Jesuits, confiscating its property. The "Casa Profesa de Isabel la Catolica," the Church at de la Flor-Street, the College of Areneros, and several other churches and Jesuit establishments had previously been destroyed by fire or demolished by the rabble.

When the elections of 16th February 1936 are over, the Popular Front, triumphant, continues its destructive work; in March the parish church of San Salvador is burnt down; in May, a bomb is placed by unknown hands in the parish church of San Miguel, the explosion causing enormous damage. On the 13th of the same month the church of San Luis is burnt down, only some few objects being rescued under great difficulties, as well as the church of San Ignacio; and on the 19th of June of the same year, after first pillaging the parish church of San Andres, they sprayed the building with petrol and set fire to it. These acts were carried out in the presence of agents of the authorities who merely looked on, making no effort to obstruct the criminals. During the days immediately following the 18th of July,

---

[2]From *The Red Domination in Spain* The General Cause, Preliminary Information drawn up by the Ministry of Justice, 1946. Bravo Murillo, 31.

1936, the red mobs invaded all the churches and convents in the city, as well as in the province of Madrid, and indeed throughout the Marxist zone; the usual method of attack consisted in surrounding the buildings and filling adjacent streets with numerous gangsters, while others penetrated into the interior and dragged out the priests, monks or nuns they found, whom they carried off, under cover of fire as prisoners. In some cases, the militia men in an attempt to justify their outrages, pretended to have been attacked by the monks; this happened in the Convento de Padres Augustinos in Valverde Street, into which they fired after having thrown live cartridges from the street into the interior of the building, by this means seeking a pretext for accusing the inmates of having shot at the militia, who then entered into the building by force, carrying off all the Augustinian Padres who were in it.[1]

"Within sixty days following the leftist-engineered elections of February, 1936, 58 political centers were pillaged, 72 public and private establishments were attacked, 45 went up in flames, 36 churches were attacked and 106 burned. Firemen trying to rescue religious works from the burning church of San Luis in Madrid were clubbed into unconsciousness. Flames devoured the statue of the Virgin before which Columbus once fulfilled his vow. The famous painting 'Virgin of Bethlehem' by Mena in Huelva, was slashed by Communist bayonets. Atrocities were multiplied. The whole of the war saw the butchering of thirteen bishops, 11,000 priests and religious, and more than 500,000 civilians. Twenty thousand churches were destroyed."[2]

WORLD WARS AND COMMUNISM ARE CAUSED BY SIN

Present day experiences clearly show that forgetfulness or negligence of Christ's presence in the world has provoked the sense of bewilderment. (PIUS XII, DEC. 25, 1955).

Our Blessed Mother at La Salette in 1846 indicated to the world, the coming of her Son at the end of time, when she told

---
[1] *The General Cause,* 1946, Afrodisio Aguado, S.A. — Bravo Murillo 31.
[2] Montague, George, S.M., *Mary's War Against Communism,* The Grail Publications, St. Meinrad, Ind., p. 7-8

the two children, "I come to tell you great news." At La Salette she wept tears of sorrow for the souls that would be lost at the judgment when He came.

Our Blessed Mother said at Fatima that "wars are punishment for the sins of the world." She also said: "If people do not heed my warning, Russia will spread her errors throughout the world." So, Communism, too, is punishment for the sins of the world.

Jacinta Marto, one of the Fatima seers, — "So many lives will be lost and most of them will go to hell." Lucia confirmed this 36 years after the apparition. She told Father Lombardi, S. J., a well known Jesuit: "Taking into account the [1953] behavior of mankind, only a small part of the human race [living at that time] will be saved." Again, Jacinta in a hospital shortly before she died gave out this warning to all scientific liberals. She said: "Pity doctors for they know not what awaits them."

Blessed Anna Maria Taigi, over a century ago, gave warning also as to the loss of souls: "The destiny of those dying on one day is that very few — not as many as ten — went straight to heaven; many remained in purgatory; and those cast into hell were as numerous as flakes of snow in midwinter." (*Vie de la V. Anna Taigi* — Page 371 — 5th Ed.)

What is causing this great loss of souls? Our Blessed Mother told us: "The sins that lead most souls to hell are sins of the flesh" — sins against the Sixth Commandment. These must be terrible sins to be punished with world wars — causing a hundred million deaths (civil and military) and worldwide Communism. And a heaven-sent cataclysm to come.

Sins against the Sixth Commandment were readily forgiven by Christ, when on earth, as were all sins when there was genuine sorrow. Such sins as murder, bank robbery or adultery are usually followed by sorrow and contrition. God readily forgives a bank robber if He is convinced the thief is determined to quit robbing banks. I do not think the sins outside of marriage against the Sixth Commandment, terrible and mortal as they are, were the worst sins Our Blessed Mother referred to. It is my opinion the sins that are causing these worldwide punishments and great loss of souls are sins against the Sixth Commandment within the marriage state. St. Augustine fifteen centuries ago declared that "Intercourse, even with one's legitimate wife, is unlawful and wicked when the conception of offspring is prevented." That has always been the teaching of God's Church.

St. Paul warns that God condemns men and women who, giving themselves up to lustful desires, "exchange the natural use for that which is against nature." (Rom. 1:26) Each Christian is bound to "possess his vessel in holiness and honor, not in the passion of lust like the gentiles who do not know God." (I Thes. 4:4,5) Those who "live according to the flesh" will meet spiritual death. Marriage must be honorable "in all things, and the bed undefiled" (Heb. 13:4).

Marital union is the most sacred of human relationships. Marital union is a potential act of co-creation with God who adds the soul at the moment of conception when a new human being is created. Any interference with such a sacred function which is consecrated by a sacrament is a very grievous matter.

Many people are of the opinion that the Sacrament of Matrimony takes place at the altar when two people exchange promises to live together as husband and wife. This is the wedding, but the consummation of the sacrament takes place when marital union occurs. If anyone on receiving the Holy Eucharist would throw the sacred host from the mouth to have it trampled upon, this would be a great sacrilege. So, also, any interference with marital union to thwart its natural effect is not only a grievous sin against God and nature, but in a sense it is a sacrilege too, for it is a desecration of that which is sacred and consecrated. God called it a "detestable thing." (Genesis 38: 9-10). Every natural use of the faculty given by God for the procreation of new human life is a sacred right with those bound in wedlock becoming co-creators.

With all sense of shame put aside, the modernist is able not only to condone but to justify this sacrilege. One large Protestant group in 1956 formally endorsed the committing of this sin which has the three requirements for being mortal sin. It is a sin of deliberation. It requires determination of the will to repeatedly perform this unnatural and esthetically repulsive act. The thwarting of this sacred function, making of it a common instrument of selfish pleasure is the cancer in present society that will cause the end of the way of life we have known in the 20th century. To refuse to cooperate in this great privilege of sharing with God in His never ending work of creation is the underlying cause of divorce, broken homes, adult and juvenile delinquency; over one million American murders yearly by married women of their unborn babes, and world cataclysms which are sent as punishment. The rejection of God's plan for human creation on such a wide scale as is practiced in the 20th century is the principal cause of much trouble in the world. Man having free will can refuse to cooperate with God — but he also must take the consequences. The proud men and women of this age of easy prosperity consider this grievous sin as something that is smart — being careful, *and there is seldom sorrow for it.* While in reality it is the sin that is bringing civilization tumbling down upon their homes, their families and themselves — to be punished by God with terrible cataclysms.

What a contrast between the uncompromising Catholic and the Pagan viewpoint on this vital subject.

The fundamental difference between the Pagan and the Catholic is that the Pagan lives only for himself and the true Catholic lives for God. All the resources of the Pagan propaganda and publicity fields are directed toward popularizing the viewpoint that MARITAL PLEASURES COME FIRST. Large families are subject to ridicule. These propagandists make it appear that the act of marital union should be under control and that the married couple should seek self-satisfaction in their exclusive interest. How intolerable it must appear to these Pagans to see Catholic couples living strictly within the true rules of the virtue of purity, rearing their unlimited families in accordance with the will of the Creator, while they are off at Palm Springs or the seashore, sunning themselves with a new mate which they casually refer to as "my present wife" or my "most recent husband."

The Catholic viewpoint: As co-creators with God, a married pair in faithfully spending their lives in fulfilling their God-given assignment of creating and maturing new human beings are able to attain close, if not indeed, perfect union with God while on earth; and thereafter being rewarded eternally with a very high place in heaven. To be one of the faithful fathers and the faithful mothers of the human race is the most noble of all God-given assignments.

THE SATANIC

Love not the world nor the things which are in the world. If any man loves the world the charity of the Father is not in him. — ST. JOHN 2:15.

We see the signs of the Antichrist in the world today. Much of what is happening all about us in mid-twentieth century is satanic. Juvenile delinquency is satanic. Much of Hollywood inspired entertainment is Satanic. At a recent National Orange Show I heard two modern business men discussing a display of so-called art as they walked away from the exhibit. "Bill, those pictures gave me the shivers. They are hellish; it is what one might expect to see walking through the halls of hell!" An excellent observation!

Jazz music, bad art and wild TV entertainment are subtle instruments which Satan uses to get a great number of good people slowly accustomed to things Satanic. The other extreme is to see the war ruins of cities of Europe which were the work of Satan on a great and horrible scale. Once prominent and peaceful cities in many countries were laid waste in great heaps of fallen masonry which covered the dead. To read about such ruins is bad enough; to see them is gruesome! Awful! No Christian can see the result of the war ruins of Europe and go away without the conviction — all that is the work of the devil.

The general evil that is in the world today is the result of Satan directing men and women in ways that will lead people away from God. Man is not clever enough, smart enough, or evil enough to bring civilization to its ruin. Such is the work resulting from diabolical leadership.

There is a well organized Anti-God force operating throughout the whole world. It is the diabolical Mystical Body of Satan. It has millions of members. It has been the ruling world force of the twentieth century. Wars, communism, revolutions and all Anti-Christ movements are manipulated by this secret society. It is determined to dethrone God in the world and, in His place, put a monarch at the head of one super-world evil government. It is their aim to build this secret society into a universal non-Christian religion to the exclusion of all others. This will accomplish their great ambition — the deification of man.

The same group in the U.S. without the sanction of Congress, put their own seal on the United States one dollar bill. Under this new seal on our currency are the Latin words: Novus Ordo Sectorum — the new order of the ages — alias "The New Deal."

EVIL SATANIC MEN MAY DESTROY THE EARTH

"A boy playing with lighted matches in a hayloft would not be in as precarious a situation as humanity finds itself today with the nations toying with the forces of titanic destruction as military leaders weigh the possibility of their use in destructive warfare. Not only is the very existence of man at stake, but he is playing with forces that *COULD DESTROY THE EARTH* itself. Unless God intervenes, unregenerated men will bring about a world catastrophe. Misuse of power is itself evil, and when it falls into the hands of EVIL men, it can only lead to destruction. Every factor present today — unless God has mercy upon us — will bring about a Twentieth Century repetition of an ancient holocaust.[1]

* * *

"While space-hopefuls and slide rule artists plan journeys to Venus and Mars, the atom threatens to blast us from our dreams and *SEAR PLANET EARTH* to a cinder"[2]

---

[1] Howard Rand
[2] John M. Scott, S.J.

Part 3

Moral Dangers

Chapter 5

Satan in Our Day

BY DOM ALOIS MAGER, O.S.B.

* A DIGEST

There are two signs which characterize the satanic: lying and murder. Lying and murder are the expression of the essence of National Socialism. Never before have they been committed so entirely for their own sake, with cold premeditation and with such complete fanaticism. Pius XI called National Socialism the *"mendacium incarnatum,"* the lie incarnate. He could not have described it more exactly.

All the information in the press, all the announcements on the wireless breathed lies. All that National Socialism said, wrote and did, was soaked in lies. National Socialism (was) built on lies. On March 21, 1933, Adolph Hitler said: "The rights of our Churches will remain unchanged. Nothing in their relation to the State will be altered. . . . The Government of the Reich sees in Christianity an impregnable basis for the work of reconstruction. It will cultivate and develop friendly relations with the Holy See." But to his accomplices he said: "I know the right way to treat these people, to get them to give way. They will bend or break, and if they are not fools they will bend. It is impossible to fight the Church; one would only make martyrs. It must be dried up. I, too, once had that fence around my soul, but I broke it, stick by stick."

The lie on which National Socialism is built up is not merely human; it is essentially Satanic. The human spirit is created for truth. In its blindness it may make mistakes; it may even defend error. But lying is not error; it is more. It is the conscious

---

*A digest of a chapter from the book "Satan," published by Sheed & Ward in 1952. Printed by courtesy of the Publisher.

[55]

ADOLPH HITLER
"Anyone against us — we kill!"
"It is not right that matters — but victory."

reversal of truth. Only spiritual beings, which is what demons are, can live essentially in the perversity of the lie. Wherever lying has become the principle of life . . . one may be sure the forces of Satan are directly at work. This was the case in National Socialism. It was satanic in its inmost nature. Its route was marked with the heaped-up bodies of murdered men.

Under National Socialism, murder was the supreme manifestation of power. Murder was a principle — a method used at every turn. Lying and murder stand for destruction and annihilation. Lying annihilates the life of the spirit, murder annihilates the life of the body.

The judgment of history has already proclaimed an unalterable verdict; one man alone was responsible for this war (World War II), with its millions of men killed on the battle-fields and its millions of murdered men, women and children — one man, Adolph Hitler, and with him his closest associates. The *Neue Zurcher Nachrichten* quotes the following horrifying statistics from a book entitled *Le Chaos Europeen:* 16,000,000 were killed in battle, 29,600,000 wounded and crippled, 3,000,000 civilians killed by bombs, 5,500,000 gassed, burnt or murdered, 24,500,000 victims of bombardments, 15,000,000 evacuated and deported, 11,000,000 in concentration camps. . . . In National Socialism, murder was a principle, a perfectly normal method used at every turn. The murder of "those who did not deserve to live" is proof enough of this.

Significantly enough, no words are reiterated so often in the speeches of Hitler as "destruction" and "annihilation." It is a fictitious power, for it is really powerless. And that is precisely the secret of the satanic. Because he is in himself powerless, the devil is a coward. I, myself, know from authentic sources — from eyewitnesses, how cowardly Hitler was in decisive moments. He left this world — a coward; or is skulking like an utter coward in some remote corner of the earth.

Canon Neuhausler of Munich, in his *Antichrist Unchained* summarizes the essence and peculiar charter of National Socialism in these words:

"There is a close connection between Satan and National Socialism.

"Satanic was the hatred of National Socialism against Christianity and all that was sacred.

"Satanic were the methods of warfare and the propaganda of National Socialism.

"Satanic were the brutality and cruelty of National Socialism.

"Satanic were the disintegration and the fall of National Socialism.

"Satanic were the murders and the murderers of National Socialism."

The spirit of National Socialism slips in everywhere, although it may present itself under different forms and in different degrees from those which it assumed in the days of Hitlerism. It is the spirit of conscious neo-paganism, which raises the three consequences of original sin to an ideal of life. Wherever this takes place, the doors are suddenly thrown open to the satanic. One power alone is capable of banishing the forces of the devil and driving them back into the pit — redemption through Christ as it operates in Christianity and the Church. Christianity and the Church have never ceased preaching to the world that salvation lies solely in the Cross — that is to say, in triumphing over the threefold consequences of original sin: the concupiscence of the eyes, the concupiscence of the flesh, and the pride of life. Only thus can the last domination of hell be finally annihilated. *"Ecce crucem Domini, fugite partes adversae."*

WHAT HAS HAPPENED TO US?
(An editorial in the San Bernardino *Sun*, Feb. 1, 1952)

All one has to do these days in order to work up a perfectly good case of cold chills is to read the daily news side by side with any history of civilization. It won't be long until the parallel between today's news stories and the sections of history dealing with the fall of the Egyptians, the Greeks, the Romans and all the other great civilizations becomes startlingly apparent — and then the chills start.

One cannot escape the fact that the decay and ultimate end of the power and glories of each of the great eras of man have been presaged first of all by a marked decline in personal and public morals. The avariciousness of the Egyptians, the amoral and immoral personal qualities of the Greeks, the political immorality of the Romans — all these immediately preceded the destruction of the civilization which those peoples had raised to such heights.

Just as inescapable is the fact that we are witnessing in the United States today the same kind of decline in personal and public morals as brought ruin to the ancients. We see it on every hand. Virtually no segment of our population is untouched by it and practically no aspect of our social and economic order is free from its evidences.

Sexual perverts have made their way into government and education. Some have been unmasked and have been ousted. Others are still in high positions. Yet, public indignation has not been fanned to the point where it can deal with the menace. Sexual irregularities are not dealt with until some child or some young woman pays with her life. Efforts to get legislation that will protect girls and children against degenerates fail to arouse any support.

Cheating and chiseling are tolerated with a shrug of the shoulders. . . The decline is very real and should be the paramount concern of every American, whether he be a private citizen or in an official position.

DANGER OF MORAL DECAY
An editorial in the San Bernardino *Sun*, August 1, 1965

"If the United States ever declines, or if this republic ever is taken over by totalitarian forces, the tragedy will occur because Americans turned their backs on morality.

"The upsurge of crime in this decade and the increasing disrespect for law and order are symptoms of moral decay. Citizen complacency and greater dependence on government portend doom for the initiative and individualism which raised this nation to its plane of greatness.

"If you aren't alarmed by the moral decay so evident in wonderful America, multiply one indifferent 1965 American by 100 million or more, and the situation becomes frightening. To eliminate the moral decay which threatens the foundations of individual freedom in this nation, there needs to be a revival of genuine Americanism — not radical extremism — which can only begin with introspection for weaknesses on the part of individual Americans. Constitutional government will not function if a citizenry chooses the role of passers-by."

* * *

The result of the decline of morality in the United States is a complete failure of some families in parts of America. In Southern California in 1965 there were two divorces for one marriage.

The explanation is a simple one. Tear the very idea of God from the hearts of men and they are of necessity urged by their passions and fallen nature to atrocious acts of all kinds. Without God there is no restraining force. With men in high government positions urged on by Godless theorists determined to de-Christianize world society, we have a result as the editor reports it. Without God man reverts to primitive barbarity.

America's manners and morals are often a reflection of Hollywood. The cinema, a useful medium for education and culture, has frequently been prostituted to undermine virtue. "Art" pictures and "adult" fare have brought the critics and indiscriminating public to the defense of plots and situations directly opposed to the ethics and morals of a decent public.

The Legion of Decency has succumbed to revised codes until "it has gone about as far as it can go." Step by step, stage by stage, nudity was introduced, violence was permitted, morals were ridiculed, the Church and the home held up to scorn, until now, thanks much to the decisions of the Supreme Court of the United States, "obscene" has no definition, pornography may not be curtailed, and the innocence of children may be dragged through the mud of sophisticated entertainment.

"Brigitte Bardot (risking the towel) ecstatically applauds the last Code revision. 'It sort of vindicates me,' she tells Bernard Vallery of the *New York Times* in a Paris interview. 'When my first shocking picture — And God Created Woman — came out, people yelled *Scandal*. (In 1957 the Legion of Decency totally condemned this film.)

" 'Later,' continues Miss Bardot, 'when my friend Jeanne Moreau's picture came out with much more daring love scenes, nobody was scandalized. . . Once the habit (nudity, adultery, etc., in movies) sets in — made in good taste, of course! — nobody will pay special attention to it!"

"Libertarians and fuzzy-minded 'progressives' who support overly-permissive attitudes on whichever front one meets them, use the same distorted terminology. Currently they parrot that sordid movie themes are essential to compassionate understanding of the human condition. They sneer at piety, deriding parents who are alarmed at lowering screen morals as out of touch with the social realities through living in a pious fog." (William H. Mooring in *The Southern Cross*, Nov. 4, 1965, p. 5)

Newsweek Magazine for November 8, 1965, called prostitution in Italy an industry that pays twenty millions of dollars annually in taxes. The article claims there are 18,000 prostitutes now walking the streets. An estimated 200,000 Italian women make their living by prostitution. In Milan alone there are 4,000 street-walkers and at least 8,000 call girls. In Rome 12,000 prostitutes stalk the avenues and streets. In Turin, 2,000; there are 9,000 call girls in that city.

One wonders if this would be the case unless it paid. And one realizes that things are probably no worse in Italy than in other countries. In England the women have been chased off the streets, but they have taken up their places in the pubs and taverns, as they have in Chicago and other American cities. Male prostitution is even more daring, prowling the streets by day and night.

The multi-billion dollar business of girlie magazines with suggestive stories and pictures, and even more pernicious ads, are protected by the courts against those worried parents and teachers who would like to save their children from the scourge.

The dissemination of birth control propaganda, sponsored even by the Government, and the daring introduction to the early stages of a drive to legalize abortions is already in the newspapers. What we have to remember is that "As man sins, so he must suffer." When the euthanasia promoters would have put to "merciful" death those with incurable diseases, God called for the able-bodied men of every nation to come into the field of battle. From that point they returned home, many with scars of battle they will never be rid of — crippled, blind, deaf, insane, or lifeless in a box. God did not take the incurables. And the same is true of the children. "Suffer the little children to come unto me." When we refuse that call, and refuse to bring children into life as God intended, we are sure to see diseases as crippling as polio, moral sickness of vandalism and delinquency, on the rise among the young. God is no ogre watching for chances to punish us. But He has placed certain eternal laws in nature, and when these laws are violated the consequences fall as surely as a stone falls when it is released from a wall. The law of gravity is no more certain or eternal than the moral laws which call for justice and punishment.

Part 4

The Day of the Lord

THE SEVEN DAYS OF CREATION
and
6000 YEARS OF TIME

GOD'S RELIGION

Year		
1	Adam & Eve	Creation
	1st Union with God	
	Original Sin	
1000		The Flood
	Period of Punishment	
2000		2000 B.C.
	ABRAHAM	
	The Chosen People	
3000		1000 B.C.
4000	JESUS IS BORN	1 A.D.
	Redemption First Resurrection	33 A.D.
	St. Peter, 1st Pope	
5000	Roman Catholic Church	
	Continues Christ's Work	
5965	570 Million Catholics	Paul VI 262nd Pope
		1965 A.D.
6000	Conquest of Antichrist Seventh Day Creation The Sabbath Era of Peace One Fold & One Shepherd Second Resurrection Last Judgment	2000 A.D.

Chapter 6

The Day of the Lord

The most difficult book in the Bible to understand is *The Apocalypse of St. John,* or *The Book of Revelations* as it is sometimes referred to. Its obscurity is due to a particular style of writing prevalent in the first century of Christianity, in which highly imaginative figures are used to concretize events, eras, and abstract truths.

Writers have presented their individual interpretations, and many have called upon *The Apocalypse* to support their belief that in the last decades of the earth's history, there will be upheavals in nature of unprecedented force, even unnatural movements of the heavenly bodies, to add to the confusion and consternation of peoples at war on earth, threatened with plagues and pestilences, earthquakes and tidal waves.

That this age of frightful cataclysms was very near seems to have been the belief already of the Apostles. When Christ described the destruction of Jerusalem his Jewish contemporaries associated that destruction with the end of the world. The good Israelite always believed there would be a universal, even cosmic, nemesis for all the trials and inflictions imposed upon them. Instead of looking for their reward in the life to come, they expected it in a kind of Golden Age here on earth, which eventually they spoke of as The Millennium or the Great Thousand Years, during which they looked for a heaven on earth.[1]

The destruction of Jerusalem was not something centuries remote. There were then living men who would witness that destruction. Hence the belief arose that the age of frightful cataclysms — associated with the end of the world — was very near.

---

[1] Feret, O.P., H.M., *The Apocalypse of St. John,* Newman Press, Westminster, Md., 1958 (See entire chapter "The Christian View of History According to The Apocalypse.")

The day of the Lord had indeed come, but in a somewhat different sense than some modern interpreters understand it.

" 'When the fulness of time was come,' writes St. Paul to the Galatians, 'God sent His Son, made of a woman, made under the law; that he might redeem them that were under the law.' (Gal. 4:4). Elsewhere he says that it was the design of God in the fulness of time to 're-establish all things in Christ, that are in heaven, and on earth, in him' (Eph. 1:10). Again the same conception of history's evolution is expressed by St. Peter in his first epistle (I Pet. 1:20), and in the admirable way the epistle to the Hebrews opens: 'God who at sundry times and in divers manners spoke in times past to the fathers by the prophet, last of all, in these days, hath spoken to us by his son. . .' (Heb. 1:1).

"For the first generation of Christians, this was the certainty on which they based their ideas of the progress of history. With the birth of Jesus, the 'end of time' foretold by the prophets had arrived. We are now in the last age of human history. Jesus himself opened His ministry by emphatically declaring 'The time is accomplished and the kingdom of God is at hand. Repent and believe the Gospel' (Mark 1:15). None of the apostles spoke in any other strain. This, indeed, was the indispensable condition of their adherence to Christ. In that Jewish environment in which they propagated their message, to recognize Jesus as the Messiah was to proclaim that the last days had arrived."[1]

When Christ foretold the "abomination of desolation" as spoken of by Daniel, He was not referring to the end of the world, but to the bringing into the sacred precincts of the temple the banners and ensigns of the Roman legions. How long the "day of the Lord" was to last, i.e., just when the judgment of God would finally come, was never known, but it was almost constantly expected. When the tribes of northern and eastern Europe poured into the Roman Empire, in the fifth and sixth centuries, the preachers of the day, Popes even, Leo the Great and Gregory the Great, spoke of the end of the world as if they believed it imminent.

Perhaps one could say that the entire theme of the *Apocalypse* can be summarized thus: The day of the Lord will open with Christ's resurrection from the dead, the "firstborn from the

---

[1] Feret, O.P., H.M., *Op. Cit.*, 87-88.

dead," and from Jerusalem disciples will traverse the earth, establishing the Kingdom in Syria, Egypt, Greece, Rome, and ultimately over the entire earth. This would not be accomplished without much opposition from the Beast, the Dragon, in the form of wars and persecutions. But in the end victory will be Christ's, and when the day of reckoning comes, He will return to earth to reward His followers.

The Jewish people, eager for a Messias who would conquer the world in their name, were unable at first to associate wars and sufferings with the conquest they expected. It is the story of the Apocalypse that though there will be crosses and obstacles, set-backs and failures, slowly against these hindrances the work of God will go on and before the end, the Church will have brought the Word of God to all peoples. Christ's prayer "That they all may be one as Thou, Father in me and I in Thee" may well be realized in the final decades of world history.

It is impossible to date any events in the *Apocalypse*, and all speculation as to the duration of the world remains only speculation. Christ has made it clear that no man knows, no angel even knows, when the final trumpet will sound.

IS THERE TO BE A MILLENNIUM?

In chapter 20 of the *Apocalypse* it is said that after the destruction of God's enemies, "the beast and the kings of the earth and their armies," with "the false prophet" and Satan himself, will be bound and cast into the pit. The saints are then to rise and reign with Christ a thousand years. At the end of this period Satan is to be loosed for a brief span...

Many of the early Christians took this as a literal description of events which would occur at the end of the world's history. Those who held to such an interpretation were known as Chiliasts or Millennarians, i.e., believers in the reign of a thousand years. This belief was common in the early Church.

After the establishment of Christianity the belief in the reign of the saints for a thousand years almost died out. St. Augustine confesses that he once held it. It appeared from time to time in the Middle Ages, and is still advocated by some of the more obscure sects.[1]

---

[1] *Addis and Arnold's Catholic Dictionary*, B. Herder Co., St. Louis, 1950.

"Christ is triumphing while all history rolls on to the glorious manifestation of that triumph in the messianic age. Since His victoriousness preeminently began with His death and resurrection, and since He did not explain to His followers that He would first ascend into heaven and then return to proclaim His triumph, they sustained the hope that onward from the time he and mankind arose again, he would, while present with them, expand His kingdom, conquer His enemies, and majestically proclaim Himself Lord of all on earth forever."[1]

"During the entire period of the messianic era on earth, symbollized by the figure of 1,000 years, Satan remains bound. Or as St. Augustine puts it: 'By the chaining of the devil is meant that he is not permitted to tempt as much as he could.' If there is a difficulty in this passage, it is in the final words of verse 3 — 'And after that he must be loosed a little while.' It could well be that John was here taking a firm stand against millennarianism, that is, the doctrine that proposed a long period of peace between the present order of temptation and trial and the *parousia*. The apostle ridicules such nonsense by letting the devil hypothetically loose to "mess up" matters. No judgment on the actuality of events, therefore, is made; and hence there is no prophecy of conditions on earth immediately preceding the parousia.[2]

In view of these accepted and scholarly interpretations of the *Apocalypse* it should be stated that I am using the term "*Apocalypse*" and "*Day of the Lord*," to describe a long period of time — from the "First Resurrection" i.e., from the redemption of the race from paganism, to the "Second Resurrection" i.e., the general resurrection at the end of the world.

However, I am conscious that even this long period of "a thousand years" must draw to a close and it is the opinion of this author that we are now in the closing days of this era. He has amassed a considerable number of prophetic sayings, some of them from saints and mystics of great weight, and it seems

---

[1] *A Catholic Commentary on Holy Scripture,* Thos. Nelson and Sons, London. "The New Testament Teaching on the Second Coming" pp. 835-843.
[2] Heidt, William, G., O.S.B., *The Book of the Apocalypse,* Collegeville, Minn., 1962 p 116

THE LAST WORLD WAR

to be a common belief of them that the twentieth century will see us in the final stages of the "Day of the Lord." How, then, can I speak of the great era of peace?

The Church did not get off to a very auspicious start, judging from the viewpoint of temporal success. Pope after pope suffered martyrdom as did the Apostles before them. Down into the underground cemeteries of Rome went the early Christians with their martyred dead, but despite ten major persecutions, the Church emerged under Constantine from the shadows and found place for her liturgy in the basilicas of Rome.

When a hundred years later the barbarian hordes threatened civilization, the Church tamed the various tribes and sent them back to their homelands to lay the foundations of twenty Christian nations.

The evils of Arianism, Nestorianism, the threat implied in lay investiture, the Albigensian heresy, the great western schism, and in the sixteenth century, the almost fatal dismemberment of the Church were indeed menacing upheavals of the Day of the Lord described in the *Apocalypse*. But one by one the Church overcame these evils, and each time the dust of battle settled, the cross of Christ stood high over the ruins, ready to reconstruct and go forward once more. It has been the history of all nations. Our own land once knew the bigotry of the Know-nothing movement and the slanders of 1928, when a Catholic first ran for the highest office of the land. The Ku Klux Klan burnt churches, too, but eventually Catholicism was the better for it. Mexico, once oppressed by a godless government, is today fervent and vigorous in religion. Portugal and Spain had their anti-clerical wars, but it has been impossible to crush out the faith. This will be the story again for Communism to learn. St. John in his first Epistle (5:19) writes: "We know that we are of God, and the whole world is in the power of the evil one. And we know that the Son of God, has come and has given us understanding, that we may know the true God and may be in His true Son."[1]

"By faith the saints conquered kingdoms, did what was just,

---

[1] More completely this theme is developed in Kurth-Day, *The Church at the Turning Points of History*, Naegele Printing Co., Helena, Mont. 1929.

obtained what was promised; they broke the jaws of lions, put out raging fires, escaped the piercing sword; though weak they were made powerful, they became strong in time of war, they turned back foreign invaders. Women received back their dead through resurrection. Others were tortured and did not accept deliverance in order to obtain a better resurrection. Others endured mockery, scourging, even chains and imprisonment. They were stoned, they were tested, they were sawed in two, they were put to death at sword's point, they went about garbed in the skins of sheep or goats, needy, afflicted, tormented. The world was not worthy of them. They used to wander about in deserts and on mountains and dwell in caves and in holes of the earth. To all these approval was given because of their faith, and they were found in Christ Jesus our Lord.

Chapter 7

A Letter from Father M. Raymond, O.C.S.O., Trappist Author

We are HIS members!   SHE is our Mother!
OUR LADY OF GETHSEMANI
Trappist-Cistercian Abbey
Trappist, Kentucky

L
G-O-D
V
E

My Dear Brother Emmett: October 11, 1951

That there is to be an Antichrist, no believer can deny. That he is to have tremendous power and cause incalculable harm is beyond question. That he is already born and on the march . . . Pius XI thought so and said so in more than one Encyclical. You think so, and say so in this thrilling book. You have good data. It could well be. If it is, you have prepared your family excellently well. If it turns out otherwise, nothing is lost.

In three great Encyclicals Pius XI has called and called the world to penance and prayer. His MISERENTISSIMUS REDEMPTOR would move a heart of stone. His CARITATE CHRISTI COMPULSI is a bugle blast for souls with any chivalry. And his DIVINI REDEMPTORIS made me weep. He was showing the great need of our day. He prophesied in those Encyclicals as truly as any of the prophets of old. The first had an Apocalyptic strain to it. The little giant of the Papacy stated flatly that the world was in the power of evil and that we were at the dawn of that day whose midday sun would see the tribu-

FATHER RAYMOND, O.C.S.O., and AUTHOR IN A KENTUCKY CORNFIELD

All Trappists are farmers. Besides being a famous author, Father Raymond is known among the Cistercians as their most versatile monk. Like Pope John, he enjoys bringing in the harvest. He is considered a mighty man on the Gethsemani farm. He loves the land and the fruits of the soil.

lations sinful man would bring upon earth by his arrogance. People were told to do what the Ninevites did — to pray and do penance. They did not listen ... The CARITATE CHRISTI COMPULSI was 'a final warning to the Nations of the World.' The Pope gave humanity its choice: 'Either it entrusts itself in humility and contrition to the benevolent powers of prayer and penance,' he said, 'or it delivers itself and the final remnants of earthly happiness to the enemy of God — the spirit of revenge and destruction.' Those are the Pope's exact words. You know the choice humanity made.

I know not exactly where Pius XI called Communism the Antichrist, but it could have been in his Encyclical against ATHEISTIC COMMUNISM. Here is something I have always used in the optimistic sense, but which I see now you can use in your Apocalyptic sense; for you can say the coming of Antichrist with the subsequent Second Coming of Jesus will be a "supernatural intervention" ... At any rate Pius XI in a private audience with Bishop Schrembs of Cleveland said: "The time is ripe, my son, for a supernatural intervention. History teaches us that when mankind has fallen lowest, when it begins to curse God and deny Him, the moment has arrived when God reveals Himself ..."

Sir Emmett, you and I both thrill to the Call of the Times. You look ahead to seeing the Second Coming ... You may be right. I don't know. I look ahead to the Face to Face Vision of God, to seeing Jesus Christ who loves me SO much, to clasping Mother Mary's hand. I care not what the step before this is: a bullet, atom bomb, gallows, sword, cancer — that does not matter — the vision after the veil falls — that alone counts. Let us both PRAY that our Babylon yet becomes Ninive — and that when the Son of Man comes He will find FAITH and CHARITY on earth! ...

You tell me you would be "disappointed if it does not materialize." You remind me of my much admired Leon Bloy — He was expecting "martyrdom and the Holy Ghost." He received neither visibly — though I think he had both invisibly.

You have done a real service to Christ and Christians. We need to think! And especially, to look upon our times as apocalyptic ... to be God-conscious and Christ-conscious, aye, to be

God-intoxicated! Faith and Fortitude are the two needs of our glorious days — and you have exemplified both in your accumulation of facts and the printing of your book. My tribute of praise and my tribute of thanks go to you in this hastily written letter.

That your desires "that all stand up whenever the Christian roll is called and shout: 'Here' . . . that your whole family become saints" I send my priestly blessing to each of the 49 and promise to lift you on my Paten until we meet in HIM who is our LIFE.

* * *

ON FARMING: Most of my days are spent in the vegetable garden for which I volunteered in late winter. Through our drought we fed the community from the garden; and now, tomatoes, corn, squash and melons. So, all in all it has been wonderful. If one wants TO BE HUMBLE — that is, to know his place in the universe — and realize God's dominance, let him FARM! I plant, I water, but it is God who gives the increase. We must have sunshine, rain and weather — and He gives them. If one wants to work hand in hand with God, LET HIM FARM!

I have worked on this Kentucky farm for thirty years. I have worked on corn, hay, soy beans, alfalfa — worked until I was dog-tired and ready to drop. A farmer is a man who helps God work out His Providence — a man who works hand in hand with Divinity, that we humans may know a harvest. Farming is the Theology of Work! We are not God conscious enough. We are not the happy people we should be. God made us to be happy here and now. Our difficulty lies in the fact that sin changes work into labor. Sin makes farming labor. Work is a dignity given man by God. [What wisdom! *Author*.]

Pray for yours in Christ Jesus,

Fr. M. RAYMOND, O.C.S.O.

Chapter 8

We Are Living in the Time of the Apocalypse

The history of the world is a succession of civilizations which have a beginning, a zenith and come to an end through some catastrophe. There once existed the Assyrian civilization, the Egyptian, the Greek, the Roman, and more recently the so-called Western civilization. All of these civilizations rose to great heights, then came to a decline when a great portion of the progress previously attained was lost. Western Civilization has been in a rapid decline morally for 50 years.

I have lived in two centuries. I was seven years old at the start of the fast-moving 20th Century. I was born on the prairies of Dakota. I saw the first automobile that crossed the Jim River to enter So. Dakota. It had wheels four feet in diameter and steel tires. It could move twelve miles per hour. My first memory was of my father taking me for fuel out on the prairie with a white mare and a blind mule hitched to a farm wagon. There was then no wood or coal in our part of Dakota. The fuel we gathered was dehydrated cattle and buffalo dung. Horsedrawn farm implements were just beginning to appear. There was no such thing as pasteurized milk and bakery bread. Clothes were washed by hand in hard water on a scrub board by the "women folks." There was no furnace heat or indoor water facilities.

And this was only 70 years ago. My ancestors were rural people, going back to St. Patrick in the 5th Century. We lived in Iowa in sod houses very much as did our forefathers 1400 years before in Ireland. There has never been a mixed marriage or an apostasy in our family history. My mother had only two terms of six weeks each in any school. We were Irish pioneers on the prairies of Iowa and Dakota with a noble heritage of loving God and adhering strictly to Catholic Culture and tradition. My grandfather sprinkled the new plowed ground with holy water as his family followed him seeding wheat, barley, and oats by hand.

In our Irish Catholic family the family rosary has been recited daily for centuries. Our ancestors came to America from the land of Saints and Scholars. The Irish people were kept humble and poor to fulfill the great destiny God had for them. God willed that the Irish live frugally suffering the persecution of the English for a *week of centuries* in order that our folks, and their neighbors could send hundreds of their sons and daughters every year to foreign lands as priests and nuns to bring Christianity to the people of the world.

Then came the 20th century with its modernism, its atheistic intellectualism, its Godless industrialism, its jazz music, pornographic literature, and many Satanic forms of entertainment. At mid-century America had become very fat with 60 million automobiles and over 60 million television sets, many other modern conveniences and bulging "fear boxes" in the basement vaults of tall buildings downtown. What does all this modernism mean?

The world will become Catholic when men become Catholic. So many American Catholics are not true Catholics today. We have been led away from genuine Catholic culture by non-Catholic materialism and intellectualism. Bishop Sheen in 1956 published the following statement in more than 100 Catholic newspapers:

"We live in apocalyptic times — we should sacrifice so that the love of God may spread to all people, before the Day of Wrath. . . . We, of the Western World, presently suffer from receiving Christ half way . . . Our Western World has not denied Christianity, it has refused Christianity. We are not Christians, but *post-Christians*."

Saint Pius X said: "We must fear that this wickedness of man is already the beginning of those evils that are to come toward the end of the world, and that the son of perdition, of whom the Apostles speak, is already on earth."

Pope Pius XI said: "These are the worst days in the history

of mankind since the deluge. . . . The time is ripe for a supernatural intervention."

Pope Pius XII said: "The world is on the verge of a frightful abyss; men must prepare themselves for suffering such as mankind has never seen."

There are only a few men who will talk on the Apocalypse. The Apocalypse is not a popular subject. The word Apocalypse is seldom mentioned. I consider this a mistake. Our people should be alerted. Our Blessed Mother does not hesitate to use apocalyptic language. A Servite priest in Chicago talks plainly on the Apocalypse. On March 5, 1954, he addressed the Serra Club of Chicago. He said: "We have a revelation from Almighty God to the effect that the *Apocalyptic Age will occur.* The Apocalypse was written by St. John the Evangelist. In it God describes in detail the punishments that He is going to send upon the world. (We have had two world wars already.) The Apocalyptic Age doesn't mean the end of the world, but when it is over *every single person in the world will be a Catholic and a saint.* Our Blessed Mother at Fatima was talking of the Apocalyptic Age when she said: "After all this is over, there will come an era of peace in which my Immaculate Heart will reign."

"I have in my possession at least 100 prophecies pronounced over 600 years ago about this catastrophe that is going to come to the world. The startling fact is that every one of these prophecies puts its finger on the age in which you and I are living. I mean the very decade in which we are living now."

For over 1900 years the true Church of Christ has been endeavoring to make the world all Catholic, but we have not been successful. We know that the world has fallen progressively into greater wickedness, with the race perverting itself more and more as it grows older. It would seem that God's idea for repopulating Heaven, by creating earth, and then man and woman to live on it, giving them free will to choose between His Father and Satan, has met with poor success.

Modern man is ill, very ill. He is sick from a disordered mind and a selfish heart. Modern man is afraid. Some of his fear has progressed to a point of desperation. Modern man has forgotten that he is superior to a machine, a balance sheet or a bank account; and because of this forgetfulness he has become an economic slave. Modern man is much more Pagan than Christian. What difference is there between many Christian business men and their Pagan competitors? And what difference is there between some professional men who profess to be Catholic, and their Pagan associates who boast of their Godlessness? We live in a secular and pagan world. The modern Christian has forgotten his destiny. He is a victim of materialism. He must be cured of this heresy before he will return to Christ's way of life, and be content to live it. We cannot find our way back to Christ, whom the modern world has rejected by merely identifying ourselves with His Catholic Church. We must influence ourselves as Christians to prevail against selfishness and greed.

Where is this modernism, which feeds off war and the preparation for more war, leading us? We pray for peace and prepare for war. Would we want peace, if we knew what Peace with Charity would do to the American way of life we are so proud of? In England a very famous editor recently wrote: "Has war been eliminated leaving Britain to go mad instead?" He implies that the modern atheistic man of materialism cannot live in peace. He MUST EITHER BE AT WAR OR "GO MAD!"

Think of it! And this condition exists not only in Britain but in any society that gives up God for the deification of man. This "madness" of Britain also exists in the United States, and in all countries where atheistic science and Godless industrialism is the force that directs the way of life. Let the modern American materialist face the fact that the present American prosperity, our bulging "fear boxes," our televisions, our flying machines and our automobiles, were all made possible by 60 years of constant preparation for war. *It has been a prosperous business.* If our prayers for peace should suddenly be answered, our war industries would be forced to shut down. If Our Blessed Mother miraculously ushered in the promised Peace it would bring Peace with charity. With the genuine peace of Christ throughout the world, war machines would become common blast furnace scrap. With the going of these demonic implements of war would also go our modern industrialized cities which grew off the production of war material. Modern man, against his will, would be forced to return to the land, and to an economy based on peace with charity. It would be the way of life Christ wished to usher into the world when He promised "peace on earth to men of good will."

Until June 28, 1950, I was a modernist, too, going about my business trying to get rich, in common with most Americans. Success and the obtaining of money was my aim. My muscles were continuously strained to the utmost. I never looked up or down — I never read — I never rested — I was always going forward toward that vague success, which we Americans love to glorify. I believed in this great American fallacy. And then for me it came to a sudden end.

Two of our sons had just graduated from a Jesuit University and one from a Jesuit High School. These sons were on a summer vacation and touring by car through Wisconsin with their mother and father. Son John was reading a Chicago Morning Tribune and he spoke up, "Dad, a new War is starting this morning. Truman is sending our boys to some place called Korea. Where is Korea, Dad?"

I did not know exactly, but answered, "Somewhere in the far Pacific."

John asked, "Why is this war being fought?"

I answered: "I do not know."

And Jude spoke up, "What was the Second World War fought for?"

And, again I answered, "I do not know, and I do not believe anyone knows the true answer to that question."

Gerald, our number seven, now a Discalced Carmelite priest, spoke up, "That is a fine kettle of fish! We spend almost a trillion dollars on a war and the people who had to fight the war know not what it was about!"

John then asked, "What did you old guys fight for in 1917, in the First World War?"

I answered, "We were told that it was a war to end all wars — to save the world for Democracy."

Everyone in the car, including myself, had a big laugh.

John spoke up again. "It seems that some group of master minds has been leading the Christian world astray — with two world wars and the terrible one in Spain now history — a new one starting today and almost one-third the world now communist — including many people in Washington, D.C."

And, then, one of the boys said, "Dad, if we must all go to Korea to fight this new war for Mr. Truman, I want to know, before I go, for what we are fighting."

I answered, "You are absolutely right! Stop the car! Turn around."

"Where to Dad?"

"We are going to find out what is behind these Satan inspired demonic world wars. Head for Dubuque and the Trappist Monastery. There are monks out there who have had time to think; men who can tell us *What Is Behind World Wars*.

My mother's folks — the Courtneys and the Sullivans met the Irish Trappists when they came up the Mississippi River to land at Dubuque back in 1849. They helped the monks build New Melleray Monastery. We have been friends of the Dubuque Trappists ever since. The Sullivans still farm the original homestead. It has been farmed continuously by the Sullivan family for over 110 years.

Arriving at New Melleray, I asked Father Abbot if he had any students of wars — "Have you anyone who can tell me what's back of world wars?"

He answered, "Oh, yes, Brother . . . and Father . . . They both have been studying the causes of our 20th century wars and the progress of the Apocalypse for many years. I will give them free time while you are here."

Soon, two giant monks came into the room assigned to me, one in a white robe — one in a brown robe.

"You want us?"

"Yes, Father, I want to talk to you about world wars. A new war of world proportions started this morning in Korea. Father, I came to New Melleray to find out what is the real cause of World Wars?"

"Sin is the cause of all Wars."

"Sin?"

"Yes, sin! If there were no sin, there could be no war. Wars are punishments for the sins of the world. There can be no Peace without Charity. The only men who can know Peace in this world are 'men of good will.' Any other questions?"

"Don't be so brief, Father. We have three days to talk on this subject."

"Of course," said the Trappist "you must realize that the world has been passing through the Apocalypse for over 100 years; and that we are rapidly approaching its end. Brother and myself expect the Antichrist may come this decade and surely before the 20th century ends."

I answered that "I know nothing about the Apocalypse except that it is the last book in the Bible. Please tell me about it. And what is meant by the Antichrist?"

This brought on the most interesting and informative discussion.

Precious books were taken from the shelves of the Monastery Library, and clippings and manuscripts too, which I never imagined were in existence. I was permitted the rare privilege of taking some of the books away from the Abbey to my home for careful study.

These Trappists changed my life. The business that I had been frantically pursuing came to be something which seemed without a worthwhile purpose. I began to read everything I could find on the Blessed Virgin Mary — and especially about her many visits to earth.

I found that the Apocalypse started in 1830 when Our Lady appeared in Paris to St. Catherine Labouré to warn France. Our Lady told this young nun, "The days are evil. Terrible things are going to happen to France. The Archbishop will die — the streets will run with blood." When asked when this would happen, Our Lady said, "within 40 years." In exactly 40 years — the Franco-Prussian War broke out.

Our Blessed Mother told this nun "world wide suffering would come in the next century." The Mother of God started off the Apocalypse in 1830 with these words:

"My child, *the whole world* will be filled with trouble and sorrow — trouble of every kind." She left the Miraculous Medal with Sister Catherine to be distributed to all the world. The Immaculate Conception was heralded by St. Catherine Labouré with this medal. The Sacred Heart of Jesus and Immaculate Mary were correlated by this medal. On the reverse side is a large "M" surmounted by a cross. Beneath the letter on the left is the Sacred Heart, crowned with thorns. A cross rises out of flames. The Immaculate Heart of Mary is to the right, pierced with a sword, and the flames rising forth. All is encircled by a diadem. St. John speaks in the Apocalypse of the "Woman clothed with the sun, the moon under her feet, and on her head a crown of twelve stars." The age of Mary had started in 1830, and so had the Apocalypse.

The Blessed Mother returned ten years later to the same house where she appeared to Sister Bisqueyburu. The Miraculous Medal and the Green Scapular are almost identical. Both are intended to save souls and to prepare Christians for suffering which would come during the Apocalypse.

Our Lady's next appearance was only six years later at La Salette, France. She appeared to two shepherd children and gave them another Apocalyptic message. She told of local punishments which would come all over Europe in the form of famine, plague and death. All Irish will remember being told of the potato famine in 1846-48 when many of our grandparents came to America. This suffering in Ireland as well as in many parts of Europe was foretold at La Salette. Part of the message applied only to Europe, but the secret message which was for the whole world told of worldwide suffering through the Apocalypse to the end of time. The message for the world was to be kept a secret until 1858. She instructed that it be then made known.

In tears, the Virgin Mary appeared to the two shepherd children at La Salette, France, and told them the cause of her grief, instructing them to tell part of her message at once, and the full message in 12 years. Popes Pius IX and Leo XIII heard these messages and believed them. However, to this day the greater part of her La Salette message is not well known. After 100 years it still is fearsome reading. It tells the wrath of God for a sinful world in words which cannot be misunderstood. In 1951 Father Gerald Culleton of the diocese of Fresno, California, published the La Salette secret message in full.

La Salette was God's second major warning. His creature, man, was wandering more and more from unity. He was marching away from the basic requirement of his social and moral nature. Following the false prophets of spiritual revolt in the sixteenth century, Christian disunity was now shaking the very foundations of society, and it has continued to do so progressively to this day.

Our Blessed Mother appeared next at Lourdes, France, in 1858. Her message was again for saving souls. "Pray for poor sinners," she said; "Pray for the world which is in such trouble. Penance, Penance, Penance!"

She appeared at Pontmain, France, in 1871, to end the Franco-Prussian War.

She then left France after five public appearances to appear at Knock, Ireland, in 1879. This appearance was most significant, for it was a silent appearance, visible to all present. Knock was an out and out figure from the Apocalypse. On this visit to Ireland Our Lady brought St. John with her. It was St. John who wrote of her, by Divine Inspiration, as the "Woman clothed with the sun, the moon under her feet, and her head crowned with twelve stars." St. John came to Knock clothed as a Bishop. He is author of the Apocalypse. At the right of the Blessed Mother stood St. Joseph, Head of the Holy Family, Patron of the Universal Church. Beside him was an altar, as it is described in the Apocalypse, the Divine Lamb standing there, a stream of blood gushing from its heart into a golden chalice. Every single thing in this apparition was Apocalyptic. *This was the sign of the times!* Had no other sign been given, this would have been sufficient to proclaim the era of the tank, the jet airplane and the atom bomb.

Then 49 years ago Our Lady appeared at Fatima. Pope Pius XII said of Fatima, "Next to the Mass, the Fatima devotions are most important."

The Fatima story is too well known for me to comment on. My message is to tell what may come after these years which God gave us to amend our lives. What is the world situation today?

When I was a boy in 1900, England was the great world giant with its Royal Navy and its proud fleet of 195 major ships — its Bank of England — its 600 colonies — its rule over a quarter of the earth — and its record of keeping Ireland poor and suffering for A WEEK OF CENTURIES.

Sixty-six years later it is all but a pauper nation. England has asked for, and received, a moratorium until the year 2000 on all interest, to say nothing of principal, on its debt to the United States. It is also now in debt to Ireland, and cannot pay up. Its proud Navy has been junked for scrap iron. The United States has agreed to send our boys and airplanes to defend the British Isles. England can no longer do so.

ENGLAND'S HOUSE OF LORDS IN 1965 VOTED TO LEGALIZE HOMOSEXUALITY AMONG MEN (the hideous sin is already legal among England's women). England thus sounded the final death knell of their country's greatness. The vote was 94 to 49 in favor of taking the step that would shove this once mighty world power over the abyss into ignoble oblivion just as early Irish Saints predicted.

And France — the beloved land of Our Lady. What has happened to her? I received a letter recently from a dear friend attached to the U. S. Embassy in Paris. I quote from this letter, "Poor France is on its deathbed, and only a miracle can save her. Some of us who love France are praying for the miracle."

Foretelling the fall of France and England, the famous Jesuit, Father Necton, said in 1772, "When England shall wane in power, the destruction of Paris will be near at hand."

The decay in Europe is the result of Godlessness during the years of the Apocalypse. It has been foretold over and over. St. Columbkille, the great Irish saint, said in 597, "Hearken until I relate things that will come in the last ages of the world. Great carnages shall be made — justice shall be outraged — great suffering shall prevail. They will plunder the property of the Church. [In Spain in 1938 thousands of Catholic churches were set on fire.] They will scoff at acts of humanity. The common people will adopt false principles, the doctors of science will become niggardly in spirit, war shall rage in the bosom of families, men shall be filled with hatred, young women will become unblushing, young people will decline in vigor. [The U.S. Army found that 50 per cent of our male youth are unable to chin themselves today.] Neighbors and blood relatives will be cold to each other, dreadful storms and hurricanes shall afflict them. After the conclusion of a long bloody rule of Ireland by England, the garment of death will descend. English nobility shall sink into humble life — wars shall be proclaimed against them, by means of which the frantically proud race shall be subdued, and will be harassed from every quarter. The English shall dwindle into disreputable people and shall forever after be deprived of power."

St. Paul in the first century said almost the same as St. Columbkille said in the 6th century. He said, "Know you this, that in the last days dangerous times will come. Men will be lovers of self, covetous, haughty, proud, blasphemers, disobedient of parents, ungrateful, criminal, heartless, faithless, slanderers, incontinent, merciless, unkind, treacherous, stubborn, puffed up with pride, loving pleasure more than God."

These two great saints were speaking prophetically on the days of the Apocalypse — the days through which we live in the 20th century. What they said bears directly upon what is happening in the world today.

In the new Commemorative Edition of the Catholic Bible, issued to celebrate the Marian Year, there is in the Foreword these words:

"In this, the twentieth century, a terrible crisis confronts the Holy Church and what still may be called Christendom. Godless men, avowedly determined to crucify Christ in His Mystical Body, are subverting not only what is Christian, but also all that is human. It is without doubt Satan's strongest assault upon the Rock of Peter and upon all that is called God."

Our Sorrowful Mother, in 1846, appeared on the mountain at La Salette shedding tears, and through Her tears said to the shepherd children, "I am here to tell you great news." Until 1917 it was not known why she should announce, "Great News" while in tears. After Fatima we realized that the "great news" she spoke of at La Salette, which she would clarify at Fatima, was the coming triumph of the church and the Second Coming of her Son. The tears were to indicate the sorrow the people of the world would suffer before her "Triumph" would be given to mankind.

Our Lady of Fatima promised: "In the end My Immaculate Heart will TRIUMPH and a period of PEACE will be granted humanity." *This is an absolute promise* without qualification. It *is certain to come.* What other "great news" could the Mother of God bring to earth other than "Peace on Earth?" The first promise of her Son at Bethlehem was "Peace on Earth." The coming of "Triumphant Peace" for the world is truly "great news."

Our Mother's promise of Peace is one of the most profound statements that have been given to mankind since Christ's ascension into heaven. This promise gives the key to what man can expect from the year 1917 to the time of the general judgment. Most people believe that this promised peace is merely a cessation of war; but it is much more than that. It will be a peace such as the world has never known. It will be peace for all humanity. It can be nothing less than ABSOLUTE peace that she will give to mankind.

The words "end," "triumph," and "period" in Our Lady's peace promise have much significance. It would seem that the word "end" should indicate the conclusion of Mother Mary's age-old struggle with Satan. The word "Triumph" should mean complete victory over evil. If the triumph is complete, this would bring the end of man's corrupt nature. If this is to be, we will soon have the reign of the Antichrist, then the second coming of Christ.

The Eschatological era is a period of time at the very end of the Apocalypse. The word Eschatological means, according to Webster: The last days of an age; the time before the end; the advent of Christ. We are in this era now.

"From a complete victory over the forces of Evil by the forces of Good will arise the most complete triumph of the Christian religion. Then will the spouse of Christ (the Church) arise strong and powerful and with great beauty, and her magnificence will shine with a cloudless brightness. All men on earth will acknowledge that the Lord alone is great; His name shall be made known by all creatures, and He will reign forever." (St. Hildegarde)

At the very last of the Apocalypse and at the end of the Bible St. John stated:

"And I saw a new heaven and a new earth. For the first heaven and the first earth passed away . . . And they will be His people, and God Himself will be with them as their God. And God will wipe away every tear from their eyes. And death shall be no more; neither shall there be mourning, nor crying, nor pain any more, for the former things have passed away."

St. John was speaking of our Blessed Mother's TRIUMPHANT PEACE — Anything short of this would be RELATIVE PEACE.

It is a great privilege to live today. These are dramatic times. Although this is an age of trouble, trial and error, and there is going to be a time of more suffering, it is also the age of Mary, and the age of Saints. For those who have a real love for the Mother of God, this century can be the happiest of Christian days despite all the wars and the constant threat of communism and atomic bombing.

These are the saints that St. Louis de Montfort said would be numerous in the last days. The thing to be convinced of is that *this is the time and to act accordingly*. It isn't something that is going to happen a hundred years from now. Many of us will take our part in one of the greatest dramas of all history — the ushering in of Our Lady's Promised Peace.

Our Heavenly Mother has been trying frantically to save us since 1830 — to wake us up.

If I am an alarmist, so also is Our Blessed Mother who opened up the earth to show Hell to the three little Fatima children so they could tell the people. She is terribly worried about the people of this world.

I want to leave this thought: It is later than we think.

Chapter 9

Second Coming of Christ As Told in The Bible

To be God-conscious and Christ-conscious, aye, to be God-intoxicated! . . . This is heaven begun before life is ended.
— FATHER RAYMOND, O.C.S.O.

There are those who do not want to see their modern way of life brought to an end. They do not want their materialistic existence upset. They want to continue to "eat, drink and be merry." These "moderns" deny that even the preliminaries to the end can ever be foretold because Jesus said that "the day and the hour knoweth no man — no, not the angels of heaven, but My Father only."

He did not say, "The day and the hour will never be known until it strikes, and I do not want it known." Christ has made the *approximate* time known to many. St. Hildegarde, 800 years ago, knew the century, but not the moment. She said, "No one can tell the moment." St. Bridget knew the approximate time; so did St. Malachy; and so did Saint Pius X.

Since the year 1800 the information has been given out. Some who were told bore Christ's stigmata and suffered His passion. In recent times very specific information was given to saintly persons in this century. I will tell of some of these revelations here. Christ gave information to His chosen ones with instructions that they tell the world. He did not want it kept secret.

Many years before the Flood came God sent Noah to give warning of the coming water. But the people did not take Noah seriously, even after it started to rain. They said to one another, "It is bound to clear up sooner or later." When God permitted Israel to be taken in captivity, warning was also given. The birth of Christ was foretold. The destruction of Jerusalem by the Romans in A.D. 70 was known in advance. So, also, the coming of Antichrist has been foretold.

"And as it was in the days of Noah, even so will be the coming of the Son of Man. For, as in the days before the flood, they were eating and drinking, marrying and giving in marriage until the day when Noah entered the ark, and they did not understand until the flood came and swept them all away; even so will be the coming of the Son of Man." — Matthew 24:38,39.

The bitter Vietnamese War, which is being fought as this is written is but a sideshow performance preceding the main event: the Last World War. This war will be different from any previous war. It will not be a war between nations, or even between men. During this war, it is said that Satan will have the power to reactivate the corpse of a dead soldier with new diabolical life so it can fight on. This war is to be the final all-out battle between the forces of Good and Evil — between God and Satan. Satan will be permitted to consistently win until the last three days — when God will put out the lights; when the only light all over the world will be from the blessed candles in the homes of the elect. In this darkness will be fought the final battle of Armageddon.

The following Biblical passages are the words of Jesus Christ, foretelling the Last Days, and the days through which we are now passing. (They also refer in part, however, to the destruction of Jerusalem.)

St. Matthew, Chapter 24: "And he, answering, said to them: 'Do you see all these things? Amen; I say to you there shall not be left here a stone upon a stone that shall not be destroyed. For nation shall rise against nation, and kingdom against kingdom: and there shall be pestilences and famines and earthquakes in places. Now all these are the beginnings of sorrows. Then shall they deliver you up to be afflicted and shall put you to death: and you shall be hated by all nations for my name's sake. And then shall many be scandalized and shall betray one another and shall hate one another. And many false prophets shall rise and shall seduce many. And because iniquity hath abounded, the charity of many shall grow cold. But he that shall persevere to the end, he shall be saved.

* * *

" 'For there shall be then great tribulation, such as hath not been seen from the beginning of the world until now, neither shall be. And unless those days had been shortened, no flesh should be saved: but for the sake of the Elect, those days shall be shortened'."

St. Mark, Chapter 13: "And Jesus answering, said to him: 'Seest thou all these great buildings? There shall not be left a stone upon a stone that shall not be thrown down. For many shall come in my name saying: I am he; and they shall deceive many. And when you shall hear of wars and rumors of wars, fear ye not. For such things must needs be: but the end is not yet. For nation shall rise against nation and kingdom against kingdom: and there shall be earthquakes in divers places and famines. These things are the beginning of sorrows.

* * *

" 'Take you heed therefore: behold, I have foretold you all things. But in those days, after that tribulation, the sun shall be darkened and the moon shall not give her light. And the stars of heaven shall be falling down and the powers that are in heaven shall be moved. And then shall they see the Son of man coming in the clouds, with great power and glory. And then shall he send his angels and shall gather together his Elect from the four winds, from the uttermost part of the earth to the uttermost part of heaven. So you also when you shall see these things come to pass, know ye that it is very nigh, even at the doors. Amen, I say to you that this generation shall not pass until all these things be done. Heaven and earth shall pass away: but my word shall not pass away'."

St. Luke, Chapter 17: "And as it came to pass in the days of Noah, so shall it be also in the days of the Son of man. They did eat and drink, they married wives and were given in marriage, until the day that Noah entered into the ark and the flood came and destroyed them all: Likewise as it came to pass in the days of Lot. They did eat and drink, they bought and sold, they planted and built. And in the day that Lot went out from

Sodom, it rained fire and brimstone from heaven and destroyed them all. Even thus shall it be in the day when the Son of man shall be revealed. In that hour, he that shall be on the housetop, and his goods in the house, let him not go down to take them away: and he that shall be in the field, in like manner, let him not return back. Remember Lot's wife."

(I John 2:18-22): "Little children, it is the last hour: and as you have heard that Antichrist cometh, even now there are become many Antichrists: whereby we know that it is the last hour. They went out from us but they were not of us. For if they had been of us, they would no doubt have remained with us: but that they may be manifest that they are not all of us. But you have the unction from the Holy One and know all things. Who is a liar, but he who denieth that Jesus is the Christ? This is Antichrist, who denieth the Father and the Son."

THE LAST HOUR

"It is the last hour" means the last age of the Church — many Antichrists, many heretics, many enemies of Christ and His Church, all forerunners of the Great Antichrist.

"They were not of us" — that is, they were not solid, steadfast genuine Christians, otherwise they would have remained in the true Church.

St. Paul's Second Epistle to the Thessalonians, Chapter 2: "Let no man deceive you by any means: for unless there come a revolt first, and the man of sin be revealed, the son of perdition who opposeth and is lifted up above all that is called God or that is worshipped, so that he sitteth in the temple of God, showing himself as if he were God. And then that wicked one shall be revealed: whom the Lord Jesus shall kill with the spirit of his mouth and shall destroy with the brightness of his coming: him whose coming is according to the working of Satan, in all power and signs and lying wonders, . . ."

"The revolt" is the falling away for over 400 years from Christ's Mystical Body — the Church. It may be supposed, too, that this falling away will increase during the days of Antichrist.

Accompanying all this is a belief that man can get along without God with new ideologies taking the place of religion. A study was made of students in large state universities, and it was found that over 50 per cent of them had lost all faith in God by graduation day. There were two devastating World Wars, and there were constant rumors of more wars. Millions of people were thrown out of their homes, and the homes destroyed. Millions of civilians — to say nothing of soldiers — were killed. Nations were wiped out. Sins against the first commandment were widespread. The lack of simple Christian charity among men, even between husbands and wives, and between brothers and sisters, was appalling. All over the earth, man's uncharitableness to his neighbor brought misery. In America, the majority of white people live out their whole lives with prejudice in their hearts for non-white minorities of our own people. Our Blessed Lady came to earth more often than ever before. She came to warn all the people on earth that such progressive Godlessness had to stop; but not over one person in a hundred, I am sure, and probably not one in a thousand of the world's population paid heed to her warnings.

It has long been my belief that some forms of cacophonous music, Hollywood and all it stands for, "Old Jim Crow," religious illiteracy, atheistic materialism in businesses and professions, that this is Satan, himself, at work winning souls away from Christ; and that those who aid him in his false philosophy are members of his diabolical mystical body.

God have mercy on the proud, obstinate self-lovers in America who, in a long lifetime, have failed to find the love of God while living in our great land which He so bountifully endowed.

THE FIRST RESURRECTION

The Apocalypse is recognized as being very difficult to understand and theologians have never fully agreed on interpretations. It has never been interpreted ex-Cathedra by the Church. The Apocalypse is now actually being enacted day by day in our times, and is, therefore, being interpreted for us. We have been aided also, by Jesus and His Mother, giving explanations through saintly mystics. The simplified version of the Bible by Monsignor Ronald Knox has helped also. In this book the 20th chapter of the Apocalypse is stated with such clarity that it becomes plain how events are to take place that will precede the end of the world. I will outline here a layman's interpretation of this 20th chapter which, of course, is also subject to error, until the Church infallibly clarifies the Apocalypse for the faithful. The following is the Knox clarification of the 20th chapter of the Apocalypse, and remarks by author.

BIBLE: "I saw, too, an angel come down from heaven with a key of the abyss in his hand, and a great chain. He made prisoner of the dragon, serpent of the primal age whom we call the devil, or Satan, and put him in bounds for a thousand years. He was not to delude the world anymore until the thousand years were over; then for a short time, he is to be released."

REMARK: It was Christ's death on the cross that caused Satan to be bound in the abyss of hell; there he was chained for at least the first thousand years, but would be, before another thousand had passed, released for a time. The thousand years he was to be bound have always been interpreted by Catholics as not an exact 1,000 years of time, but rather an indefinite but prolonged period. Satan, as Lucifer, is to be released at the time Antichrist is released.

Sister Catherine Emmerich said about the year 1800: "In the center of hell I saw a dark and horrible looking abyss, and into this Lucifer was cast after being strongly bound with chains; God, Himself, had decreed this (after Christ died on the cross) and I was told . . . that Lucifer will be unchained for a time, 50 or 60 years before the year 2000. A certain number of demons are to be let loose much earlier than Lucifer in order to tempt men. I should think that some must be loosened even in the present day."

Therefore, Lucifer has been bound from the year 33 to our present time, when he will be loosed. That time may already have begun, culminating in the 1260 days of the reign of Antichrist.

BIBLE: "Then I saw thrones prepared for those to whom judgment was committed; I saw the souls of all who went to execution for love of the truth concerning Jesus, and of God's word, and all who would not worship the beast, or its image, or bear its mark on their foreheads and their hands. These were endowed with life, and reigned with Christ a thousand years. But the rest of the dead remained lifeless while the thousand years lasted. Such is the FIRST RESURRECTION."

REMARK: This, I believe, applies to the Old Testament saints who it is thought arose and ascended with Christ into heaven. This would be the "first" resurrection among them in glory are now the martyrs of the era of Christianity.

BIBLE: "Blessed and holy is his lot who has a share in this First Resurrection; OVER SUCH THE SECOND DEATH HAS NO POWER, they will be priests of Christ; all those thousand years they will reign with him in heaven."

REMARK: This applies to those who remain alive during all the days of Antichrist and who are to be clad in immortality without ever experiencing death. (St. Paul's first epistle to the Thessalonians.) It is the humble opinion of this lay writer that at that time will be the period of Peace promised by the Mother of Christ in the year 1917 in Fatima, Portugal, when she said: "In the end my Immaculate Heart will triumph and some time of Peace will be given to humanity." It is to be the time of the One Fold and One Shepherd. It is the time of the triumph of the Mystical Body of Jesus Christ on earth.

BIBLE: "Then when the thousand years are over, Satan will be let loose from his prison, and will go out to seduce the nations that live at the four corners of the earth."

REMARK: This could well be the chaotic conditions now forming in preparation for the great show down.

BIBLE: "That is the meaning of Gog and Magog — and muster them for battle, countless as the sand by the sea. They came up across the whole breadth of the earth and beleaguered the encampment of the saints, and the beloved city. But God sent fire from heaven to consume them, and the devil, their seducer, was thrown into the lake of fire and brimstone, where like himself, the beast, and the false prophet will be tormented days and nights eternally."

REMARK: This is the final chaining of Satan and his cohorts.

BIBLE: "And now I saw a great throne, all white, and one sitting on it, at whose glance earth and heaven vanished, and were found no more. Before this throne, in my vision, the dead must come, great and little alike, and the books were opened. Another book too, was opened, the book of life. And the dead were judged by their deeds, as the book recorded them. The sea, too, gave up the dead and hell gave up the dead they imprisoned, and each man was judged according to his deeds, while death and hell were thrown into the lake of fire. THIS IS THE SECOND DEATH; everyone must be thrown into this lake of fire, unless his name was found written in the book of life."

REMARK: This is the Last Judgment for all those who died during all the ages up until the time of Antichrist. Those who are to be exempted from the Last Judgment are only the Elect who suffered the crucifixion of the Mystical Body, those "priests of God, and priests of Christ; OVER SUCH THE SECOND DEATH HAS NO POWER — blessed and holy is his lot who has a share in the FIRST RESURRECTION." This will be the final end of the world.

THE DEATH OF THE MYSTICAL BODY

It could well be that the crucifixion of the Mystical Body of Christ will follow the pattern of the crucifixion of His human body on Calvary. For each day He suffered His private passion, the crucifixion of the Whole Body may be for one year's time instead of one day's time, as on Calvary. The 1260 days of the reign of Antichrist may be the 3½ years of public passion of Christ's whole church on earth. As His private passion progressed, His suffering increased. At 3 o'clock on the second day when He died on the cross His physical human life ended and His dead body was placed in a tomb. He rose from the dead at His resurrection but remained on earth in a glorified state for 40 days, and then ascended into Heaven.

What will happen to man during the passion of His Mystical Body? What will happen if the corpse is to remain in the tomb for 1½ years, instead of 1½ days, as on Calvary? If it is true that the Mystical Body is about to go into its passion under Antichrist, we can well ponder the possibility of the Mystical passion following the pattern set by Christ's own passion on Calvary.

Of course, the visible Church and the Mystical Body of Christ are identical and indefectible, which means "the gates of hell shall not prevail against her." Theoretically the analogy is attractive, but theologically it might not be sound. It would seem, however, that Christ died in His human nature when His body was separated from His soul and lay in the tomb, as the Divinity of Christ could never die; and neither will His Mystical Body be dead when It is invisible on earth while in hiding underground (in its sepulchre) during Its crucifixion. It will be dead only as Christ was dead during His personal crucifixion. Just as Christ could never be extinct, neither can His church. As Bishop Sheen said in 1948, "It is the very nature of God to exist. . . . If at this moment we are going into the catacombs, it is only as Christ went into the grave. What we are witnessing is the death of an era of civilization, but not the death of Him."

As the time progresses through the 1260 days, so would our suffering increase as it did for Christ. The whole Mystical Body would die and be laid in a sepulchre to remain there for 1½ years. Those who would die at the hands of Antichrist would rise from their graves and from out of the sea to ascend into the air to join those who remained alive and who were clad in immortality without death. "And the dead who are with Christ shall rise first . . . then we who are alive (on earth), who are left, shall be taken up together with them in the clouds to meet Christ, into the air." . . . I Thes. 4:15-17. "And the souls of them that were beheaded for the testimony of Jesus and for the word of God and who had not adored the beast nor his image, nor received his character on their foreheads or in their hands; and they lived and reigned with Christ a thousand years. The rest of the dead (those who died before Antichrist and did not take part in the crucifixion of Christ's Mystical Body) lived not till the thousand years were finished." Apocalypse 20:4-5.

The thousand years mentioned by St. John though usually taken to mean the entire Christian era, may be the time of peace promised by Christ's own Mother at Fatima. This promised peace can well be compared to the 40 days Christ remained on earth after His crucifixion. And after the crucifixion of the whole Body of Christ's Church, we may remain on earth, too; and the full elect of God will then ascend into Heaven at the time Christ will complete the Universal Judgment of all those who died before Antichrist; and then will come the end of the world. "Blessed and Holy is He that hath part in the First Resurrection" — Apoc. 20:6.

THE END OF THE WORLD

In Dr. William Thomas Walsh's book, "Our Lady of Fatima," is found, in the Epilogue, these words taken from a conversation between Dr. Walsh and Sister Maria das Dores, on the afternoon of July 15, 1946. Sister Maria is Lucia — one of the shepherds of Fatima.

Dr. Walsh: "Have you had any revelation from Our Lady about the end of the world?"

Lucia: "I cannot answer that question."

It is my interpretation that the third Fatima secret has to do with the end of the world. If not — Lucia would have answered Dr. Walsh's question with a natural and simple "No."

Late in 1952, while at work on the third printing of this book, we were able to add the following profound information: We now find that Jacinta, one of the three Fatima children, reported that Our Blessed Mother said:

"IF PEOPLE DO NOT AMEND THEIR LIVES THE WORLD WILL END."

There are people everywhere who have come to the conclusion that the end of the world may come with atomic bombs. Other signs of the times consistently support such a belief. To have it confirmed by authority from heaven is breath-taking. These words of Jacinta become a most important part of the complete Fatima message mankind received from Our Lady of the Rosary.

When Jacinta was asked by Fr. Farmegao, shortly after the miracle of the sun, "What did the Lady say this last time — (Oct. 13)?" He received this answer: "The Lady said:

" 'I have come to tell you that people must not offend Our Lord anymore because He is very much offended and that if the people amend their lives THE WAR WILL END, and if not THE WORLD WILL END.' "

This is reported by a priest who spent seven years at Fatima. Archbishop Cushing of Boston said of him in a foreword to his book: "Father De Marchi has earned an international reputation as an authority on the apparitions of 1917." In the fall of 1952 Father John De Marchi, I.M.C., published his book: "The Immaculate Heart." On page 163 and again on 164, he twice states these words of Jacinta: "If people amend their lives the war will end, and if not the world will end."

WE KNOW THE CHOICE HUMANITY MADE!

From WANDERER, November 4, 1966

An impressive event is told in the life of Pope Leo XIII. The Pope had gone to meet with some of his Cardinals. Suddenly he sank down as if in a faint; the Cardinals thought he was dead. But after some time he awoke and said: - "What a horrible picture I was given to see; what the coming times would bring, - the misleading powers and raving devils in all countries fighting against the Church. In the nick of time St. Michael appeared again, and cast Satan and his cohorts into the abyss of hell." It was then the Pope wrote that prayer which we used to say after Low Mass: "St. Michael, the Archangel, defend us in battle." Regretfully it has been discontinued, but I hope you are still saying it privately. . . . We have reason to "Put on the armor of God" to resist Satan. Some recent Popes and Saints have warned us that the antiChrist will appear about the year 2,000; he is already born. WATCH!! — (MOST REV. WILLIAM L. ADRIAN, Bishop of Nashville, September 22nd, 1966.)

Chapter 10

The Coming of the Dreadful Antichrist

Since the dropping of atomic bombs on Japan, and since reading that Russia, England, and the United States are stockpiling atomic bombs, all people have thus been put on notice that grave impending evil casts a shadow of doom over the whole earth.

We have had one demonstration of the power of destruction of atomic energy. After Hiroshima, men set to work to make the most of this terrible force — to find other ways it could be used in war for wider and more complete destruction. Years later we have "in the works," meaning in production, the following means to use the atomic phenomenon for greater destructive purposes: air force weapons, hydrogen bombs, atom powered aircraft, pilotless aircraft, radioactive dust, atomic missile ships, carrier based atom bombs, atom powered submarines, atomic torpedoes, atomic mines, atomic howitzers, atomic guided missiles, and radiological gas and dust. Then there is the equally deadly chemical warfare department and the bacteriological field, producing through chemistry more instruments of destruction.

We are told this production is to safeguard Peace — that our enemies will fear our power and not bring on war. Nonsense! War is brought on by Satan. War is punishment for sin. We have always had the means to cause death in war, and especially since gunpowder was discovered — and wars have not decreased, but have increased in numbers and deadliness. Fear of death never stopped war or maintained Peace. Peace comes with Virtue; and in no other way.

We read of the atrocities in Korea and later at Viet Nam and throughout the whole of the Communist-dominated areas which, as this is written, cover nearly one-third the populated areas of the world. We all know that highly developed forces of destruction will be used. We tremble at the thought of what it means.

Only a few people actually realize that something entirely different than a repetition of World Wars One and Two is in the making. We think our war preparation is to win one more World War. But what hangs over us is a "theological matter." It is God's wrath that is about to descend on a wicked world. The fact that a great apostasy, not merely a heresy — but a widespread atheism has been growing all over the earth, makes any thinking person who believes in God acknowledge, to himself at least, that the great evil described by the Apostles is about to descend on the world. This punishment is spoken of many times in the Bible. We are told it will take place toward the end of time, preceding the end of the world. The term "last hour" has meant the last age of the Church of Christ. It is almost too overwhelming a thought for some men and women in the world today to believe we are to be actors in the greatest drama in the history of man. This writer believes that these Biblical warnings are soon to be realized.

The term Antichrist has been often understood as being a reference to a group or movement, that stands in opposition to what Jesus Christ stands for, and denies God. This opposition is found in individuals and institutions. St. John the Apostle wrote that there were already heretics who denied the Incarnation. The pagan Roman empire and its priesthood worshipped false gods and were viciously anti-Christian.

ANTICHRIST HAS BEEN BORN

The author feels that there is convincing evidence for him to accept as truth that the Antichrist was born on February 5, 1962, and by this writing should be approaching four years of age. At this early age, it is said, he appears to be preternaturally precocious.

This opinion, based on numerous writings would seem to be confirmed by the recent experiences of an American woman, Mrs. Jeane Dixon, of Washington, D.C., who has given evidence of a rare gift of clairvoyant perception. She claims to have witnessed by remote perception the birth of a baby boy in the

Middle East, who, she says, is destined to play an important role in the future history of nations.[1]

The antichrist that is to precede the coming of Christ is to be a man born of woman and diabolically possessed. An eminent theologian has given us an excellent description of what the antichrist will be. Father Francisco Suarez, S. J., Doctor Eximius, a great Jesuit who lived 1548-1617, held, in Disputation 54, "De Mysteriis Vitae Christi," that:

I. The Antichrist is a certain and determinate man (section i).

II. The Antichrist will be lord of the world for three years and a half (section ii).

III. The Antichrist will be a Jew by race and religion. This is very probable, as it is affirmed by St. Jerome, St. Ambrose, and many other Fathers (section ii).

IV. The Antichrist will be possessed by the devil from the beginning of his conception. He will be a pretender and false prophet (section iii).

V. The first dogma and fundamental principle of Antichrist will be TO DENY THE DIVINITY AND RELIGION OF CHRIST; he will pretend to be the Messiah; he will be the adorer and servant of the devil; he will be an atheist. The Antichrist will spread his superstition by the following means: 1) Persuasion and eloquence; 2) the liberal distribution of riches; 3) fear and threats; 4) signs and prodigies (section iv).

VI. The Antichrist will obtain rule by force and fraud. He will begin in Babylon and will be monarch of the whole world. His capital will be Jerusalem (section v).

VII. The persecution of the Church under the Antichrist will be the most bitter of all persecutions; it will be both temporal and spiritual. 1) He will oblige men to deny Christ; 2) to abandon all worship of God; 3) to renounce the true God and to render worship to no supreme Deity, but only to a mortal man, the Antichrist. In this persecution perhaps the greater part of

---

[1] Ruth Montgomery, *A Gift of Prophecy, The Phenomenal Jeane Dixon*, Wm. Morrow and Co., Inc., New York, 1965.

the faithful will be separated from Christ. The Antichrist WILL DIE BY THE SPECIAL POWER OF CHRIST (section vi).

"Before the Antichrist attacks men by force he will join to himself some partisans . . . And this fraud will consist not only in falsity of doctrine . . . but also in temporal promises . . . his fraud will consist in enormous riches . . . and with splendid donations he will attract to himself an infinite multitude of people, for it is said in Daniel 2:43, that he will be the lord of treasures of gold and silver and of all the precious things of Egypt. This is what leads Anselm (in the "Elucidarius") to say that, by the industry of demons all hidden money will be manifested to him, both in the sea and in the farthest limits and recesses of the earth. More yet, perhaps even the minerals of gold and silver, elaborated by the power of demons, will be all offered to him and used by him to obtain his empire" (section 5).

"Suarez (after St. Jerome, St. Ambrose, Sulpicius Severus, et al.), says that Antichrist shall be born of Jewish extraction, and will profess the Jewish religion; not through real devotion, but through hypocrisy, in order more easily to persuade the great majority of that mysterious race to receive him as their Messiah. He will have two important objects in doing this. In the first place, he will thus obtain the enthusiastic support and the wealth of the Jews, and through this material advantage be able to open the way to his ambition for high dignities and human power. The opinion of these Christian writers is derived from the following words of the New Testament. Our Divine Lord and Saviour said to the Jews: 'I am come in the name of my Father, and you receive me not. If another (Antichrist) shall come in his own name, you will receive him.' (St. John 5:43) St. Paul also says: 'He whose coming is according to the working of Satan, in all power and signs and lying wonders, and in all seduction of iniquity to them that perish, because they receive not the love of truth (Jesus Christ) that they may be saved; therefore God (in punishment of it) will send them the operation of error (Antichrist), to believe a lie.' (Thess. 2:9-10) Our Divine Lord and Saviour Jesus Christ was born from the Jewish race, and, preaching to them the truth, confirmed it with many incontestable miracles, yet they obstinately refused to believe in Him or His doctrines. Antichrist shall be born from the same people, who will allow themselves to be deceived by his satanic power, signs, and lying wonders, and will enthusiastically RECEIVE HIM AS THEIR LONG-EXPECTED MESSIAH. Thus we see how obstinacy in error leads men to greater crimes and to final reprobation. Because they receive not the love of truth, that they may be saved; therefore God sent them the operation of error to believe a lie."

* * *

Another renowned theologian of the Redemptorist order, Father Michael Muller, C.S.S.R., gave us in the year 1884, probably the best description of Antichrist and his reign that is of record.

ANTICHRIST
By Michael Muller, C.S.S.R.[1] — 1884

The story is told of a Western-bound train, flying along with lightning speed: The time was shortly after sunset. Suddenly a crash was heard. The train stopped. "What is the matter?" the passengers asked one another. A huge owl, dazzled by the glare, had struck against the headlight at the front of the engine, severed the glass, and tried to extinguish the light; and a great bull had set its head against the oncoming engine, to stop the train. The lamp was rekindled, the engine sped on, but the stupid owl and the bull were cast aside, dead, and left to rot, and be devoured by wild beasts. An Irishman, on seeing them, exclaimed: "I admire your courage, but condemn your judgment."

This train may be likened to the holy Catholic Church, speeding on, on her heaven-sent mission, to lead men to heaven by the light of her holy doctrine. The foolish owl, the enemy of light and the friend of darkness, represents Lucifer, who, as the Foe of God, and of the light of God's holy religion, has always been endeavoring to extinguish the light of the true religion. The bull represents the kings and emperors, the heretics

---

[1] This article was published by B. Herder, St. Louis, in 1886. Permission to reprint from B. Herder Co.

and members of secret societies, whom Lucifer uses to stop, if possible, the progress of the Catholic Church, the bearer of the light of faith. Although it is hard, in a certain sense, not to marvel at the courage of Lucifer's agents, yet we cannot but condemn their judgment, their folly and wickedness, in opposing the work of God, and bringing down upon themselves the everlasting curse of the Almighty.

Satan has, indeed, been engaged, from the beginning of the world, in doing all in his power to entice men away from God, and to be himself worshipped, instead of the Creator. The introduction, establishment, persistence, and power of the various evils, revolting superstitions of the ancient heathen world, or of pagan nations in modern times, are nothing but the work of the devil. They reveal a more than human power. God permitted Satan to operate upon the Gentiles for their hatred of truth, and their apostasy from the primitive religions of the holy patriarchs and prophets. Men, left to themselves, to human nature alone, however low they might be prone to descend, never could descend so low as to worship wood and stone, four-footed beasts, and creeping things. To do this needs Satanic delusion.

The state of irreligion and infidelity in which the greater part of mankind is plunged is but the work of Satan. How could men, without Satanic delusion, be impious enough to make liars of Jesus Christ, of the Holy Ghost, of the apostles; to blaspheme the mother of God, and God's saints; to slander the spouse of Jesus Christ, the Roman Catholic Church, in every possible manner; nay, even to deny the existence of Almighty God? They could not fall so low, without diabolical influence.

The enemies of the Catholic Church have always proved false prophets. They have asserted, again and again, that even the inventions of modern times would weaken her hold upon the world: and these very inventions serve only to elucidate the truth that is in her, and to increase and to strengthen her power.

"The printing press," they said, "will surely weaken her authority."

"Steam," they cried, "will so change society, that the old decrepit Church of Rome, that great obstacle on the railroad of materialism, will certainly be run over, and cast aside as the worn-out and useless wreck."

"The telegraph," said our enemies, "will give so rapid an impulse to the development of civilization, that the slow, ancient ways of the Catholic Church will be derided and rejected." But here again the inventions of man become the willing handmaids of the Church. The grace of God so overrules the inventions of man, and the powers of nature, that even the terrible lightning becomes the vivid messenger which flashes the blessing of Christ's Vicar unto all lands.

One event that will take place before the end of the world, as a prelude to the last days of the human race on earth, is the appearance of that extra-ordinary person, Antichrist. St. Paul the Apostle admonishing the Thessalonians not to give way to terrors, as if the last day was at hand, assured them that the last day would not come "till there came a revolt, first, and the man of sin be released, the son of perdition, who opposeth, and is lifted up above all that is called God, showing himself as if he were God." (2 Thess. 2:3,4) By "the man of sin, the son of perdition," all Christian antiquity and the subsequent ages have ever understood that superlatively wicked man, to be Antichrist.

But when is Antichrist to come? God has appointed the time for the arrival of the son of perdition. But "no man can tell the moment," says St. Hildegarde (1098-1179) "when Antichrist shall make himself manifest to the world; the angels even know it not (in the 12th Century). But this manifestation will be, as it were, a parody of the incarnation of the Divine Word. Christ came neither at the beginning nor at the end of time. He came toward evening, at least when the heat of the day was declining. What happened then? He opened the marrow of the law, and gave vent to the great floods of virtue. He restored to the world virginity in his own person, that the divine germ, impregnated by the Spirit, might take root in the hearts of men. The homicide (Antichrist) also will come suddenly; he will come at the hour of sunset, at the time when night succeeds day."

If we consider the general decay of religion which now (1884) prevails, if we see how little the practice of morality is attended to, how little even religion is thought of, we cannot help thinking that mankind has already made gigantic progress toward that apostasy, as St. Paul calls it, or toward that general defection from the faith, that degeneracy of morals, which will take place before Antichrist, the great minister of Satan, appears. How swift, indeed, must be the decline of true faith, while free-thinking, religious indifferentism, infidelity, and godless education of the young, grow at such a pace; while every one seems to accept as a fixed principle to believe nothing more than his reason comprehends, or what coincides with his own private humor! What practice of morality can be expected from people who are immersed in wordly pleasures, or in pursuits of private interests, in the gratifications of their shameful passion of lust; who never spend a thought about eternity, or scarcely ever address their God and Creator in a short prayer?

When a tide of irreligion and infidelity has broken in, and is seen to swell in volume day by day, [with a climax in 1966], what wonder if the period approaches when God will bring all to the test, and try them as metal in the fiery furnace, in order to discriminate between the good and the bad, and to separate the sound from the unsound grain? Hence St. Hildegarde exclaims: "O ye faithful! Listen to this testimony, and preserve it in your memory as a safeguard, so that terror may not find you unprovided, nor the man of sin, taking you at unawares, drag you to perdition. Arm yourselves with the weapon of faith, and prepare yourselves for a fierce battle. Keep close to the Divine Word, and follow His steps, who appeared on this earth not with the pomp of gorgeous ostentation, but in the most profound humility."

The unparalleled success which will attend the arms of Antichrist, the greatness of his power, and the extent of his dominion, beyond everything that the world has ever seen before, will strike with amazement the whole human race. "And all the earth was in admiration after the beast; and they adore the beast saying: Who is like to the beast? And who shall be able to fight with him?" (Apoc. 13:4.) Thinking himself all-powerful, Antichrist will acknowledge no superior in heaven or on earth. With this conviction, he will proceed to the temple of God which he will enter, and there, extolling his own supreme authority, his dominion, his unlimited power over everything, proclaim himself God, and ordain divine homage and worship to be paid to his person.

This we learn from St. Paul, who says that "the man of sin, the son of perdition, is lifted up above all that is called God, or that is worshipped, so that he sitteth in the temple of God, showing himself as if he were God." (2 Thess. 2:3,4.) He will forbid any other deity to be acknowledged but himself, and prohibits all worship of the Supreme Being, all exercise of the Christian religion, and particularly the holy sacrifice of the Mass, because in it Christ is personally present and adored as God. All this has been foretold by the Prophet Daniel. (Dan. 8:11; 12:11.) The Holy sacrifice of the Mass will not be offered up publicly for three years and a half, and the abomination unto desolation is set up; that is, the abominable worship of a man is set up in the place of that of God. (Matt. 24:5,16.) A most cruel persecution will be raised by Antichrist, to force the worship of his pretended divinity upon the world. Henoch and Elias, and other holy men, will appear and admonish the people not to believe in Antichrist, and that his reign is to last but for three years and a half.

On finding that many refuse to pay him divine honor, Antichrist will first try to win them over by persuasive methods. For that purpose he will avail himself of the power which the dragon (Lucifer) gave him of working false miracles. By the help of the devil, then, Antichrist will perform many prodigies and give extraordinary signs, "whose coming," says St. Paul, "is according to the work of Satan, in all power, and signs, and lying wonders." (2 Thess. 2:9.) In the "Revelations" of St. Hildegarde, we read that the "magical art of Antichrist will simulate the most wonderful signs: he will disturb the air; he will produce thunder and tempests, horrid hail and lightning; move mountains, dry up rivers, and clothe with fresh verdure the barren trees of the forest. By his deeds he will exercise influence over all the elements, over dry land and water; but he will put forth his infernal powers chiefly over men. He will seem to restore health, and take it away; he will drive away demons, and restore life to the dead. How shall this be? By sending some possessed soul into the corpse, there to remain a short time; but these sorts of resurrections will be but of a short duration."

Dazzled and bewildered by such wonders, many will begin to waver in their faith, and will be seduced to worship this mock god: "There shall arise false Christs, and false prophets, and shall show great signs and wonders, insomuch as to deceive, if possible, even the elect." (Matt. 24:24.) But Christ, who is never wanting to His Church, will interpose His power to baffle that of the devil and Antichrist. He will invest many of the Christian preachers, particularly Henoch and Elias, with extraordinary miraculous powers. As Moses and Aaron were sent by the Almighty to contend with Pharoah and his magicians, and to rescue the Israelites from slavery, so will Elias and Henoch be the two chief messengers whom Christ will employ to oppose his enemy, Antichrist, and to preserve His elect from falling into his snares.

And as the magicians of Egypt, with all their demoniacal charms and incantations, were vanquished by the signal superiority of the miracles of Moses and Aaron, so will the prodigies of Antichrist be eclipsed and confounded by the far greater number and splendor of the miracles of Elias and Henoch. "These my two witnesses shall prophesy one thousand two hundred and sixty days, clothed in sackcloth. If any man will hurt them, fire shall come out of their mouths, and shall devour their enemies. And if any man will hurt them, in this manner must he be slain. These have power to shut heaven, that it rains not in the days of their prophecy; and they have power over waters to turn them into blood, and to strike the earth with all plagues as often as they will." (Apoc. 11:3,5,6.) When the powers of the Almighty and of Satan come in collision, the power of Satan must certainly disappear. Hence those only will be deluded who wilfully shut their eyes to the clear light of evidence and so we are informed by St. Paul in his epistle to the Thessalonians: "Whose (Antichrist's) coming is according to the working of Satan in all power, and signs, and lying wonders, and in all seduction of iniquity to them that perish; because they received not the love of the truth, that they might be saved. Therefore, God shall send them the operation of error, to believe lying;

that all may be judged who have not believed the truth, but have consented to iniquity." (2 Thess. 2:9-11.)

Antichrist, seeing all his wonderful operations baffled by the shining evidence of Henoch's and Elias's miracles, and perceiving that multitudes of Christians refuse to acknowledge his godhead, swells with anger; and being actuated by Satan, who possesses him, he arrogantly boasts of his preeminence over all other men that have ever existed, of the greatness of his empire, of the number of his armies, of his command over all the beings and works of nature, and he even presumes to extol his own power above that of the Almighty. (Apoc. 13:5; 2 Thess. 2:2-4.) Daniel says: "He shall think himself able to change times and laws" (7:25). He will imagine himself powerful enough to change the course of times and seasons of the year: as night into day, winter into summer.

Not having been able to gain many Christians, he now, in rage, flies in the face of heaven; he blasphemes God, revolts against Him, blasphemes His name and religion, heaven, the angels, and saints. He will deny that the Son of God became man; he will deny all the truths of religion: "He shall speak words against the Most High One." (Dan. 7:25.) His power will extend over every nation and people of the globe: "And power has been given him over every tribe and people, and tongue and nation." (Apoc. 13:7.) Already monarch of a great part of the kingdoms of the earth, he will subdue the rest, and tyrannize over all mankind, and persecute religion in every corner of the earth. Then, such a general apostasy of mankind will take place, that, except the elect, all the rest will yield to the tyranny of Antichrist, and adore him as God: "It was given unto him to make war with the saints, and to overcome them. And all that dwell upon the earth adored him, whose names are not written in the book of life of the Lamb." (Apoc. 13:7,8.)

Antichrist will now have also an associate of the same stamp as himself, who will be his principal minister and chief aid in his future proceedings. (See Apoc. 13:11-18.) Finding himself so powerful by Satan's aid, and seconded by so able a minister, his false prophet, as St. John calls him; while, on the other hand, he sees the converted Jews and other Christians refusing him divine homage, and so fortified by the exhortations and miracles of their teachers, that all his pretended wonders can make no impression upon them, he resolves to compel them by force into compliance, to show no mercy to the refractory, but to destroy them, and utterly wipe out the Christian name. So, by his immense army, he carries destruction through every nation that refuses to worship him as God.

Almighty God having prepared his servants for the combat, permits Antichrist to carry on the most bloody war that ever took place since the existence of the world, in which will be slain the third part of men. (Apoc. 9:15.) This war will last three years and a half. The persecution will prevail over the whole world. For it shall be permitted to Antichrist and his agents to tread under foot the Holy City, the whole body of Christians, for three years and a half. This space of time Christ has set apart to purify His Church, and try the patience and faith of His servants. (Apoc. 13:9,10.)

The general calamity of the times will be such, that, while Antichrist spreads abroad a gloom of desolation and slaughter by his army, and thus becomes the instrument of punishment to the wicked, he will exercise at the same time a most bloody persecution against the servants of God. Hell and earth combine; the devil, Antichrist, and the false prophet, confederate together to extirpate Christianity. They set all engines at work, to abolish all worship of God, and to establish idolatry. The barbarous tortures employed in the primitive persecutions are to be revived, and new ones, yet more cruel, invented. The racks, gridirons, fire, and other instruments of torment, will be reproduced, and the Christians dragged before the statue of Antichrist, to refuse to adore, which is certain death. (Apoc. 13:15.) Antichrist, being now in his full career of power, will crush the saints of God. (Dan. 7:25.) In this connection, read how Antiochus Epiphanes treated the Jews (2 Mach. 5:6), and a faint idea will be furnished of the cruelties of Antichrist.

But on account of the weakness of human nature, these times of most disastrous tribulation will be shortened; they will last for only three years and a half, out of regard for the faithful servants of God. (Matt. 24:21,22.) The Lord will also send St. Michael, the Archangel, to fight the powers of hell, and assist the faithful. (Dan. 12:1.) He will give to His servants extraordinary graces, to enable them to stand their trials; He will encourage them by the constant preaching of His holy ministers, who will perform great miracles, and convert many to the Lord.

The Church, therefore, at this period, though in appearance so much oppressed, will shine more gloriously than in any former age, by the number of Christian champions, who will not fear to make open profession of their faith; who, by their invincible fortitude, will baffle all the arts and defy the torments of Antichrist, and who will soar in triumph to heaven, bearing the crown of martyrdom. Antichrist, having borne down all opposition, is now at the summit of his power; he is the greatest monarch the world ever saw, being conqueror of the whole earth. He has compelled a great part of mankind to pay him divine honor, he has sacrificed an immense number to his rage and jealousy.

Some of the Christians, however, will not fail to admonish Antichrist of his impending fate. Enraged at hearing from the expiring Christians, the supreme decree which dooms him, with all his followers, to be destroyed by Jesus Christ and his celestial army, he resolves to make war against God himself. (Apoc. 16:13,14.) He invites all kings and potentates to engage in this war against God. As Satan in the beginning made war against God, so now he urges Antichrist and his associates to do the same. Intoxicated with pride and power, and stimulated by Satan, he pursues his resolution to suffer no rival, but to contend for superiority with the Sovereign of Heaven. Condemning what he had heard from the Christians, that all power shall be wrested from him by Christ, and he himself be laid in the dust, he proposes to cope with Christ and all His heavenly attendants, by a proportionable army, assembled from the whole earth by the three evil spirits that had been sent for the purpose, to engage all potentates in this war with heaven.

But, unhappy being! The time which God has fixed to his dominion is drawing to a close. The three years and a half are expiring. The Lord is about to execute judgment upon the numberless nations gathered together. And when He shall come down to execute His judgments upon these armies, the sun and moon shall be darkened, and the stars shall withdraw their shining, and He will pass over Jerusalem with a dreadful noise that will strike them with terror and dread. (Isaiah 34:1-4; Apoc. 6:12-14.) The enemies of God will try to hide themselves, and say to the mountains and rocks: Fall upon us, and hide us from the face of Him that sitteth upon the throne. (Apoc. 15:15-16; 19:11-21.) At the terrible appearance of Christ descending through the skies with His army, His enemies are struck with consternation; and by His order, Antichrist is seized and made captive, and with him the great imposter, the false prophet. Christ, with the sole breath of His mouth, hurls down Antichrist alive into hell-fire. (2 Thess. 2:8.) Immediately after, his whole army is slaughtered. (Zach. 19:1-7; Isaiah 14: 3, 7, 19.) And those who have escaped yet, but who have been guilty of idolatry, will be overtaken in the same way by the wrath of God. (Apoc. 14:10-11; Jer. 25:15, 30-33.) Thus all abetters of Antichrist will be slain all over the world. (Jer. 66:24.)

From such a victory over its enemies, rises then the complete triumph of the Christian religion. "Then," says St. Hildegarde, "will the spouse of Christ (the Church) arise strong and powerful with wonderful beauty, and her magnificence will shine with a cloudless brightness. All will acknowledge that the Lord alone is great, His name shall be made known by all creatures, and He will reign forever."

Chapter 11

The End of the World? No . . . Not Yet!

As I write this chapter, I wish to make an emphatic clarification. The end of time, as referred to throughout this book, does not mean the end of the world and the general judgment. More properly, it means the end of one important period of time, or the end of our present era. It means, for this writer, the end of the First Resurrection, which started when Christ was crucified on the cross and rose from the dead. This period of the First Resurrection will end after long years of confusion and evil. These long ages the author expects to end about the year 2,000, when the very sinful twentieth century ends — after a period when many people lost all sense of morality. It is this long sinful history of the world that the author expects will end — this murderous century, when men killed their fellow men by the millions, justifying the murder in the name of war. All this sinfulness, I believe, is to stop as the twentieth century comes to an end. It is the time when the Seventh Millennium will set in, and will be the day of the Sabbath in the plan of creation.

The day when the Sabbath starts will be the coming of the time of peace — the time of the One Fold and One Shepherd. It will be the time when there will be an answer to our daily prayers: "THY KINGDOM COME — ON EARTH." It is to be that period of time promised by the Mother of God in 1917 when she said: "In the end my immaculate heart will triumph and a period of peace will be granted humanity."

Of course, all Christians who believe the Bible is the true word of God are of the opinion that the world will end some time. Very few believe, however, that this will come in our time, and that they will take a part in this great drama. Since the year 1914, when I was a boy of 21 years, and when men started butchering one another in World War I, it has been my belief that the end of the world is not far away. This murderous slaughter has continued all through the Twentieth Century and is taking place in 1966.

It has been the common opinion among Jews, Gentiles, and Latin and Greek Christians, that the present evil world will last no longer than 6,000 years after the day of creation. The end of this long period of time will be up in 35 years. Before the end, antichrist will be released.

January, 1960, was the time set by our Sister Lucy to release the Fatima secret. The world was anxiously awaiting the last part of the Fatima message. No doubt, Pope John had good reason in not making it public. It probably was fearsome reading. In my opinion it has to do with the remaining days of the Twentieth Century, including the reign of the Antichrist and the end of time before year 2,000. And saintly Pope John knew the world was not ready for such an announcement. The Fatima Secret could well have been . . . "prepare for the end." Pope John did exactly this. Almost immediately after January 1st, 1960, he set about to organize the Ecumenical Council to accomplish a spiritual renovation of the church. The real purpose behind this great gathering of the hierarchy of the world in Rome could only be to undo world-wide Christian disorder and the falling away resulting from 400 years of Protestantism.

As current events are reported daily, all of us who love our native land must realize that we Americans are rapidly losing our dear country. We see one-world government advocates in public office with dangerous subversives from our own and other lands making great progress toward such a government. This Godless government as planned would be the world of Lucifer, disguised under the name of liberalism. Seeing this, we must realize that the reign of the Antichrist will come with this kind of atheism; that Antichrist will be the ruler of this one-world organization. The leaders and promoters of this demonic movement are precursors of Antichrist; precursors leading the way for the coming of the false Messiah.

It is because of the overwhelming one-world movement that I am reprinting this book. This new printing will explain the real cause behind a one-world government. It will explain at

THE COMING OF THE YEAR 2,000 A.D.

length why the desire for dethroning God throughout the world is basically the result of satanic leadership.

Christians and Jews, from the beginning of Christianity, and before, have taught that 6,000 years after the creation of Adam and Eve, the consummation will occur. The period after the consummation is to be the seventh day of creation — the Sabbath, which will bring on the "ONE FOLD AND ONE SHEPHERD" and the time of peace promised at Fatima OUR BLESSED MOTHER'S TRIUMPHANT PEACE.

St. Jerome said, "It is common belief that the world will last 6,000 years." St. Gaudentius said, "Truly holy days will come after 6,000 years of time have passed."

Assuming that our evil world shall last no longer than 6,000 years, as has been the common opinion and expectation of humanity reaching back into antiquity, we then have only 35 years remaining until the end of time, as we have known it.

The exact year when Christ was born is not known. There is no agreement that it was exactly Year One. Time has consisted of 2,000 years in the law of nature, following the creation of Adam and Eve; 2,000 years followed in the law of Moses; and 2,000 years were allotted for the law of Jesus Christ, which started at the Year One, A.D. Of the 2,000 years in the Christian Era, 1965 years have passed. When talking about the end of time, Christ said to His apostles, "And unless those days be shortened, there should no flesh be saved; but for the sake of the elect, those days shall be shortened." Matt. 24:32. This shortening of time seems to be a vital matter for our Divine Lord. On reading His carefully selected words about the end of the world, we must realize that this shortening of time will be important. We may conclude that a considerable number of years may be deleted. Today's rapidly moving current events are proof of His concern. How many days will be shortened? How many years, less than 2,000, will come the end? One per cent deduction of time would be 20 years. One per cent of time seems little enough. This would reduce the remaining years to 17.

But wait a minute, Culligan: Christ said, "the day and the

hour knoweth no man — no, not the angels of heaven, but My Father only." Matt. 24

Correct! He referred to the last day and the exact hour — the day when the final consummation will occur. It seems to be His plan that the coming of the end will take all people by complete surprise. "The day of the Lord will come as a thief." 2 Peter 3:10. But He does want us to know the approximate time. He wants to prepare all for His coming. Pope John and Pope Paul are following His wishes: — to prepare the world. He was asked by His disciples, Matt. 24:3, "Tell us what will be the signs of Thy coming, and the consummation of the world." He gave several signs to watch for. Christ said:

   I. "You will hear of wars and rumors of war." Matt. 24:6 Surely, this prophecy of Our Lord has been totally fulfilled. All this century there have been wars — hot wars and cold wars — and constant rumors of wars.
   II. "There will be earthquakes in places — these things are the beginnings of sorrow." Matt. 24:7-8

I can give personal assurance that this prophecy has been fulfilled. We Culligans had our personal earthquake, which occurred in 1959. A geologist of the United States placed the epicenter of the great Montana earthquake, which shook the earth for 200 miles diameter, in the Culligan front yard. It toppled over a whole mountain, filling the beautiful Madison River Canyon, covering 30 campers with millions of tons of rock. Yes, — there have been earthquakes — many of them. On Our Lady's Feast Day, August 15, 1950, the most extensive and destructive quake in the history of man struck in Asia at noon. This quake was referred to as "when the world exploded." There have been terrifying physical convulsions of many types the past ten years — floods, tornadoes, and especially typhoons. Yes, this prophecy has been fulfilled.

   III. "And the Gospel of the kingdom shall be preached in the whole world and *then shall the consummation come.*" Matt. 24 — Luke 21

We now have missionaries preaching the Gospel to all nations. I asked a question of Reverend Lawrence G. Mack, S.V.D., former Provincial of the great Missionary Society of the Divine

Word. "Is the Gospel being preached to all nations?" He answered, "We have our own priests preaching the Gospel, not only in every nation, but also among the tribes of primitive people all over the world. There are many other religious orders with their priests and nuns working beside us. The answer to your question is: Yes."

IV. "Yet, when the Son of Man comes, will he find, do you think, faith on the earth?" Luke 18:8

There has already been a great falling away. It started 400 years ago by a tremendous act of rebellion on the part of Catholics, which started Protestantism. Let me emphasize: It was Catholics who started Protestantism that has resulted in the 266 different so called Christian religions in America today. This was "the great falling away" of the Bible. Besides Protestantism, we have other present day falling away from the Rock of Peter. This is due to marital entanglements, and many other forms of modernism of which Catholics are victims. Yes, the falling away of the Bible has long been a reality.

V. There is, however, one Biblical occurrence to be fulfilled before the consummation can occur. We must yet have the antichrist. "The day of the Lord will not come unless the apostasy comes first, and the man of sin is revealed, the son of perdition, who opposes and is exalted above all that is called God, or that is worshipped, so that he sits in the temple of God, and gives himself out as if he were God." (2 Thes. 2:3,4)

EARLY IRISH SAINTS FORETELL LAST DAYS
St. Malachy

We have the following words of St. Malachy — the archbishop of Armagh — one of the great Irish saints:

St. Malachy predicted, in year 1130, "My beloved native Isle will undergo, at the hands of England, oppression, persecution, and calamities of every kind during ONE WEEK OF CENTURIES. But she will preserve her fidelity to God and to His church amidst all her trials." This prophecy was fulfilled to the letter. Ireland suffered terribly, to the start of the twentieth century. This suffering proved providential, and for a most important reason. Suffering, prayer and study makes for saints. Ireland has long been known as the home of "saints and scholars." For hundreds of years, no public mass was permitted in Ireland. Of course, there were priests in hiding to say private and secret Mass. The Irish women recited rosaries almost constantly. This suffering of Irish people trained and prepared religious for foreign lands. Today, in California, most of the secular priests in parishes and nuns in our hospitals were born and trained in Ireland. For many hundreds of years, during the WEEK OF CENTURIES, thousands of religious — nuns and priests — left their homeland in Ireland for the missions throughout the world, and are still doing so today in great numbers.

LIVES OF THE ROMAN PONTIFFS FROM YEAR 1130 TO THE END OF TIME

St. Malachy named all the popes from the year 1130 to the end of time. St. Malachy was another of the saints who knew that time will end about year 2,000. He said there would be 268 popes from his day until the end of time. On St. Malachy's 1966 schedule, we will have four more popes to follow Paul. He may reign only a short time. In this event there would be only three remaining popes to follow Paul. The average reign of all the popes throughout the centuries has been seven years. Including Paul's, and three more full reigns to follow for an average of seven years, gives a total of 28 years to the end. St. Malachy's prediction that the end will come before year 2,000 seems to be correct.

ST. COLUMBKILLE

It has been foretold in 597, by St. Columbkille, another great early Irish saint: "Hearken until I relate things that will come in *the last ages of the world*. Great carnages shall be made — justice shall be outraged — great suffering shall prevail. They will plunder the property of the Church. They will scoff at acts of humanity. The common people will adopt false principles, the doctors of science will become niggardly; war shall rage in the bosom of families; men shall be filled with hatred; young women will become unblushing; young people will decline in vigor. Neighbors and blood relatives will be cold to each other, dreadful storms and hurricanes shall afflict them. After the conclusion of a long bloody rule of Ireland by England, the garment of death will descend. English nobility shall sink into humble life — wars shall be proclaimed against them, by means of which the frantically proud race shall be subdued, and will be harassed from every quarter. The English shall dwindle into disreputable people and shall forever after be deprived of power."

St. Paul, in the first century, said almost the same as St. Columbkille said in the sixth century. He said, "Know you this, that in the last days dangerous times will come. Men will be lovers of self, covetous, haughty, proud, blasphemers, disobedient of parents, ungrateful, criminal, heartless, faithless, slanderers, incontinent, merciless, unkind, treacherous, stubborn, puffed up with pride, loving pleasure more than God. Ever learning yet never attaining knowledge of the truth; — but they will make no progress, for their folly will be obvious to all." (2 Tim. 3:1-9).

These two great saints were speaking prophetically on the days of the apocalypse — the days through which we have lived in the 20th century. What they said reads directly upon what is happening in the world today.

ONE WORLDISM AND INTERNATIONALISM
Satanic Inspired Current Signs of Approaching End

In the womb of time there is breeding a race of men who shall be my total servants. — LUCIFER

"For it shall be permitted to Antichrist and his agents to tread underfoot the whole body of Christians, for three and one-half years. This space of time Christ has set apart to purify His church and try the patience and faith of His servants." — Apocalypse 13, 9-10

On reading current newspapers and magazines, it is certain that this time for "patience and faith" has started. To all American Christians who see the coming of atheism on a broad scale — who have seen our Supreme Court making formal and final decisions to dethrone God — surely, the need to "purify His church" is leading in that direction, with the coming of

Antichrist not far away. Much of what is happening in the 20th century is Satanic. Man on his own, corrupt as he is, is not evil enough to have brought civilization to its present condition. Our un-Godly way of life is the master work of Satan. Our wealth, our prosperity, our easy living, our Godless public educational system, our entertainment, is all a part of his subtle plan to lead man to choose wealth and other forms of materialism ahead of Christ's humble plan of simple living, while we await our kingdom in the next world.

In 1950 Bishop Fulton Sheen said about Antichrist and his false faith:

"The Antichrist will not be so-called, otherwise he would have no followers. He will wear no red tights, nor vomit sulphur... He will come disguised as the Great Humanitarian; he will talk peace, prosperity and plenty... He will foster science, but only to have armament makers use one marvel of science to destroy another... He will even speak of Christ and say that He was the greatest man who ever lived... In the midst of all his seeming love for humanity and his glib talk of freedom and equality he will have one great secret which he will tell to no one: HE WILL NOT BELIEVE IN GOD."

It seems that the birth of the Antichrist was delayed 97 years by God. The Blessed Mother told the two shepherd children at La Salette, in 1846, about the coming of the Antichrist. The boy, Girard, as a part of his secret message, said: "The monster will arrive at the end of the 19th century." The girl, Melanie Mathieu, said the following lines were a part of the secret message she received: "In the year 1865, the abomination will be seen in holy places — convents, etc. It will be about this time (1865) that antichrist will be born."

However, Antichrist did not come as foretold at La Salette. The delay could have been to obtain more souls for the communion of saints. Rafaelo Cardinal Merry del Val said, during World War II: "All soldiers who die on the battlefield after offering their lives for their country will go as martyrs straight to Heaven." It would seem that the number of martyrs from two world wars, plus all natural deaths in 100 years, of Christians who love God, would reach more than a billion souls.

It is the opinion of the author that the 1960 Fatima Secret, which has not been released by either Pope John or Pope Paul, is fearsome reading — like the Secret of La Salette — and that the Secret of Fatima also tells of the coming of the Antichrist in the latter days of the 20th century. And it was because of such frightening information that our latest two popes would not release it.

OUR LADY FORETOLD "FLYING SAUCERS"

In the summer of 1947, one of my sons interested me (author) in what has become to be known as "Flying Saucers." Since then I have read much on the subject; but my mind did not set into an opinion until I found a book describing the landing of one of these so-called spaceships near San Diego, California. It was seen by six reputable citizens to emerge from a much larger strange appearing cigar-shaped mother-ship and come to earth, and an aviator alight from it. A conversation, lasting one hour, is said to have followed between a man from the planet Venus and one of these six people from earth. It was then that I made up my mind that "Flying Saucers" are not manned by human beings from other planets, but that they are operated by aviators from the Air Force of Satan; and that the whole strange unexplained phenomenon of "Flying Saucers" is one of the diabolical wonders that Our Lady warned would come with Antichrist.

WORDS FROM THE MOTHER OF GOD
IN HER LA SALETTE SECRET - 1846

"After this, the devil will be possessed of such power that those who are not firmly established in Me will be deceived. Together with Antichrist, THE DEMONS WILL WORK GREAT FALSE MIRACLES ON EARTH AND IN THE AIR."

Astronaut scientists have told us that there is only water and water vapors on planet earth in the solar system, and that all other solar bodies, including our moon, are completely water-free. Therefore, human life, animal or planet life, can live only on earth. There can be no humans on any of the solar planets, such as Venus, to fly saucers to earth.

Prophets and Prophecies

RT. REV. MSGR. WILLIAM C. McGRATH, P.A., S.F.M.
Director, Pilgrim-Virgin Fatima Tour, which took the statue of Our Lady of Fatima into 42 states over a period of 30 months.
—1947-50

The following is taken from his book, "Fatima or World Suicide," Imprimatur, March, 1950, by Ruffillus J. McVinney, S.T.D., Bishop of Providence, R.I.:

* * *

World events are heading inexorably towards an apocalyptic climax. Two ideological worlds, whose objectives can never be reconciled, are moving towards a head-on collision, whose resounding impact may well mean the end of the thing we call civilization. Two world wars have driven the little people almost to the point of despair, and a third could mean the extermination of the greater part of the human race. In spite of the patent hypocrisies of diplomatic parlance, it becomes increasingly obvious that the "objective" of one world is the end of Christianity — the complete, utter destruction of everything and, if necessary, every person standing in the way of the realization of that plan. The challenge of Antichrist has been hurled in the face of the Christian world and that challenge will never be met by the force of arms.

Is America geared to meet this challenge? It can be met only by a return to God; and it is idle to pretend in the few years that may be left us, before the final madness, we may expect a wide-spread sincere return to the Christian way of life. There will be a soul-searching, intensive, sincere return on the part of an enlightened few. The others will not change their ways until they are forced by fearful war, or heaven-sent disaster.

It is senseless to wring our hands over the bland folly of politicians and diplomats while we, ourselves, are sinning against the light. Too many empty-souled Christians, serenely oblivious of eternity, are evaluating life in terms of things material. But God will not be forgotten — when love fails to win the hearts of men today, then God will make use of other means to bring wayward stiffnecked humanity to its senses. Yet — in the sinister shadow of apocalyptic destruction, the leaders of nations continue to assemble and the diplomatic game of "make believe" goes on.

America is now morally sick unto death, and not all the atom bombs or supersonic planes will avail to save her if men do not turn back to God. The Mother of Jesus hurries around the world, warning against the current deluge of impurity. There are millions in America who are habitually guilty of abominations that would bring a blush of shame to the cheek of an honest pagan.

One cannot but be impressed by the disquieting unanimity of prophetic warnings concerning the days that lie before us. Pope Pius XII, when gloriously reigning, not given to melodramatic statement, describes OUR TIMES AS THE DARKEST DAYS SINCE THE DELUGE, and speaks of punishment such as humankind has never known. He said: "The hour has struck — the battle, the most widespread, bitter and ferocious the world has ever known, has been joined. It must be fought to a finish."

Around the middle of this century has been singled out in literally hundreds of prophecies as the time when the forces of Antichrist will rage. Are all such prophecies to be thrown aside because the sophisticates of this "enlightened" age have such supreme contempt for THE PEOPLE OF SIMPLE FAITH WHO TAKE THEM SERIOUSLY? Shall we be saved now by the "careful" approach of the research director, or the professor or, for that matter, the theologian?

The Blessed Mother, when she tries to save the world appears to people of simple faith and, for the most part, to little children. This divine predilection for illiteracy, for those who have eyes to see, is an indictment of our academic promiscuity.

ST. THOMAS SAYS
In His Summa

"In all ages men have been divinely instructed in matters expedient for the salvation of the elect . . . and in all ages there have been persons possessed of the spirit of prophecy, not for the purpose of announcing new doctrines, but to direct human actions."

This means that private prophecy, while not binding on anyone as to acceptance, has a function, and an important function in the lives of men. It certainly is a part of Divine Providence, and, as St. Thomas says, this is not reserved to those alone who prophesy. It would seem, from the Saint's words, that men will always need some private revelations to aid them in attaining their goal. The fact is that in all ages there have been persons in the Church, most of them saints, who have received what is understood as private revelations, and these have been of advantage to all men.

I will now give a few of the many private revelations referred to by Msgr. McGrath, relating to our time, and let the reader judge of their aptness.

ST. BRIDGET OF SWEDEN (d. 1373)

"The time of Antichrist will be near when the measure of injustice will overflow and when wickedness has grown to immense proportions, when the Christians love heresies and the unjust trample underfoot the servants of God.

"At the end of this age, the Antichrist will be born. As Christ was born from the highest type of womanhood, so Antichrist will be born from the lowest. He will be a child-wonder at birth. His mother will be an accursed woman, who will pretend to be well informed in spiritual things, and his father an accursed man, from the seed of whom the Devil shall form his work. The time of this Antichrist, well known to me, will come when iniquity and impiety shall above measure abound, when injustice shall have filled the measure to overflowing, and wickedness shall have grown to immeasurable proportions. Before, however, Antichrist arrives, the gate of Faith will be opened to some nations, and the Scripture shall be verified. Hence, when many Christians will be lovers of heresies, and wicked men will persecute the clergy and trample spirituality and justice under foot, THIS SHOULD BE THE SIGN THAT ANTICHRIST SHALL COME WITHOUT DELAY.

"Lastly, he shall arrive, the most wicked of men, and, helped by the Jews, he will fight against the whole world; he will reign during three years, and shall have dominion over the whole earth; he will make every effort to abolish from the earth the Christian name, and very many Christians shall be killed."

ST. LOUIS de MONTFORT (d. 1716)

"The training and education of the great saints, who will appear towards the end of the world, is reserved for the Mother of God. These great saints will surpass in holiness the majority of the other saints as the cedar of Lebanon surpasses the lowly shrub. These great saints, full of grace and zeal, will be chosen in order to oppose the enemies of God who will appear everywhere. By their word and example these saints will bring the whole world to a true veneration of Mary. This will bring them many enemies, but also much blessing.

"The power of Mary over all devils will be particularly outstanding in the last period of time. She will extend the Kingdom of Christ over the idolators and Moslems, and there will come a glorious era in which Mary will be the ruler and queen of human hearts."

PROPHECY OF AN OLIVETAN MONK

In the year 1720, while some Italian laborers were digging near the city of Viterbo about forty miles from Rome, they found a grave containing an entire incorrupt body, dressed in the habit of an Olivetan monk, holding in his right hand a well-preserved manuscript, that nobody could remove from his grasp. It is not known how long the monk had been in his grave. The news of this discovery having been immediately communicated to the abbot of a neighboring monastery, he hastened to the spot indicated in company with several of his religious, and in their presence and that of many other persons he commanded the dead monk, in virtue of holy obedience, to give up the paper, which was immediately done. The abbot, having opened it, read in it the following predictions, which were faithfully copied, the original being forwarded to Pope Clement XII in Rome, where is was also copied by several high ecclesiastics and other persons. It is from one of these authentic copies that we publish the following:

1. From the year 1760 to 1770, America shall be on fire. (Correct. This prophecy has relation to the American Revolution.)

2. From the year 1770 to 1780, great earthquakes on the Rhine. (Correct.)

3. From the year 1780 to 1790, faith shall pass away. (Correct. Faith was poisoned in France and other neighboring countries by the writings of Rousseau, Voltaire, Diderot, D'Lambert.)

4. From the year 1790 to 1800, the Church of God shall bleed. (Correct. First French Revolution.)

5. In the year 1800, the pastor shall not exist. (Correct. Pius VI was captured by the French revolutionary government and made a prisoner at Valence.)

6. From the year 1860 to . . . God's wrath over the whole earth. (Correct. 100 years of wars.)

7. For the year 1890: All nations come and adore God. (Incorrect. To have occurred under the Great Monarch who was delayed by God.)

8. From the year 1940 to 1950, the victim and the sacrifice shall cease. (Correct. No Mass in much of Europe under Stalin.)

9. After the year 1950 there shall be the abomination of desolation. (Correct. The Last World War started in June, 1950, in Korea and the Viet Nam war in 1965 . . . Atomic bombs.)

JANE LE ROYER (d. 1798)
SISTER MARY OF THE NATIVITY

"Many precursors, false prophets, and members of infernal secret societies, worshippers of Satan, shall impugn the most sacred dogmas and doctrines of our holy religion, shall persecute the faithful, shall commit abominable actions; but THE REAL AND EXTREME ABOMINATION OF DESOLA-

TION SHALL MORE FULLY BE ACCOMPLISHED DURING THE REIGN OF ANTICHRIST, which will last about three years and a half.

"Thereupon I saw a great power arising against the Church. It despoiled, plundered and laid waste to the vineyard of the Lord, made of it a foot path for those passing over it, and derided it before the nations as an object of scorn and mockery. After desecrating the celibate and suppressing monasticism, this power boldly confiscated the properties of the Church and at the same time usurped the powers of the pope, whose person and laws they condemned.

"You will soon become aware of a great transformation. For the end has not as yet set in and they have not as yet reached the goal, as they suppose. To be sure, the dawn begins to break, but the age that follows will be stormy and full of suffering.

"Woe, woe, woe TO THE LAST CENTURY which is descending! What tribulations precede its commencements.

"Out of this mighty voice I recognized that these woeful tribulations will make their appearance in the age before the judgment. And as I pondered over and weighed, in God, the last century, I saw, that which BEGINS WITH 1800 WILL NOT YET BE THE LAST.

"I see that when the Second Coming of Christ approaches, a bad priest will do much harm to the Church.

"When the time of the reign of Antichrist is near, a false religion will appear which will be opposed to the unity of God and His Church. This will cause the greatest schism the world has ever known. The nearer the time of the end, the more the darkness of Satan will spread on Earth, the greater will be the number of the children of corruption, and the number of Just will correspondingly diminish.

"Antichrist will kill the Pope, probably by crucifixion. As a child of ten he will know more than anyone else in the world and when he is thirty he will begin his real work.

"The day of retribution will now begin, because, being full of the spirit of Lucifer, with the greatest presumption and self love he will consider himself God, and in his haughtiness he will endeavor, together with his followers, to solemnly arise to Heaven to the throne of God. The Almighty has already prepared St.

Michael with power and justice and charged him to oppose Antichrist in the heavens. When the demon group with Antichrist in their midst arrives, St. Michael will descend from Heaven with great speed upon them, being filled with holy indignation. With his appearance great fear surges through the proud army. A terrible voice sounds from the mouth of St. Michael as the earth opens: 'Begone you cursed! Down into the deepest abyss of Hell!' A bolt of lightning from the cloud casts Antichrist and his cohorts into the fearful abyss of fire and flames with such force that the deepest foundations tremble and all Hell resounds. With the fall of Antichrist will come severe earthquakes, thick darkness will cover the Earth."

SISTER CATHERINE EMMERICH

This nun was a poor Westphalian girl, born in 1774, who became an Augustinian religious at Dulmen and died in 1824. Her book "The Dolorous Passion" has taken its place among the most famous of the visions recorded in Catholic spiritual writings. In this book, in her description of Hell, she states: "In the centre of Hell I saw a dark and horrible looking abyss, and into this Lucifer was cast, after being strongly bound with chains; God himself had decreed this and I was told . . . that Lucifer will be unchained for a time, 50 or 60 years before the year of Christ 2000. A certain number of demons are to be let loose much earlier than Lucifer, in order to tempt men. I should think that some must be loosened even in the present day (1802-1824)."

The Bishop of Munster introduced the cause of the beatification of Sister Emmerich in 1892. She was a stigmatist.

MATTHEW LANG (d. 1820)

"After the Great war [World Wars I and II] there will be no peace. The people will rise and all will fight against each other. . . The rich and nobles will be killed. THE WORLD WAR WILL NOT MAKE PEOPLE BETTER BUT MUCH WORSE. . . Tell your children that their children will live to see the time when the earth will be cleared. God will do away with people because there will be no charity among men. Religious faith will decline; priests will not be respected; people will be intent only on eating and drinking; there will be many immensely rich people and large numbers of paupers; great wealth will not endure long, for the red caps (Communists?) will come. People will hide in the forests and many will go into exile. After this civil conflict and general clearing up, people will love each other as much as previously they hated one another."

FRANCISCAN FRIAR OF MT. SINAI (d. 1840)

"A terrible war will break out throughout Europe; they will tear each other to pieces and blood will flow in streams.

"Spain and Portugal both have to efface a debt of blood, partly because of the inhumanness with which they conquered America, murdering so many thousands in a cruel manner, all because of vain gold, and partly because THEY CAPTURED SO MANY INNOCENT PEOPLE IN AFRICA, ALL IMAGES OF GOD, AND SOLD THEM INTO SLAVERY LIKE CATTLE.

"England, this country of merchants WHICH SUPPORTS ALL INJUSTICES FOR THE SAKE OF GAIN, will become the scene of the greatest cruelties. Poverty will come and all colonies will sever themselves from England.

"Italy, Italy, thou beautiful country! I cry over thee! A part of your prosperous cities will be destroyed; here so many Germans find their grave.

"Blessed years will then again make their appearance, and THE YEAR 1957 WILL HEAL ALL WOUNDS. Blessed are they who live to see this year."

SISTER BERTINA BOUQUILLION (d. 1850)

"I have seen the holy patriarch Henoch, one of the two just men who shall have to fight against Antichrist, and sustain the faithful during their severe trials at the end of the world. He was dressed like a missionary, ready, as it were, to start for his great approaching difficult mission; the end of the world.

"The coming of Antichrist will be unobserved by most people.

"The end of time is nearing and Antichrist will not delay in coming. However, neither we nor those sisters who come after us will see him, but those who come after them will fall under his reign. At the time of his coming nothing will change in this house. All will be in its usual order. The religious exercises, the work, the occupations in the wards — all will be done in the customary manner, when suddenly all the sisters will be aware that Antichrist is master of the world. The beginning of the End will not come in the nineteenth century BUT CERTAINLY IN THE TWENTIETH CENTURY."

ST. ANSELM — 1109

The Apostles of Jesus Christ, while preaching the Holy Gospel will endure suffering and privations whereas the apostles of Antichrist will want for nothing; they will have worldly treasure in abundance to reward them who accept his teachings... While Antichrist reigns he will prohibit under pain of death the offering of the Holy Sacrifice of the Mass. Mass will again be said in forests and in secret places as was in the first days of Christianity... The Jews will expect the Messiah to restore Jerusalem to its greatest glory. Antichrist will command that Jerusalem be rebuilt in splendor and will order his palace to be built there. [See page 101 this book.]

ST. HILDEGARDE — 1179

The Son of Perdition will come when the world loses its stability at the end of time. At Antichrist's birth great confusion will prevail on earth.

ST. PAUL — 2 THESS. 5:3

St. Paul in the first century, warned that when people demand Peace and Security, the second coming of Christ is at hand.

MOTHER SHIPTON — ENGLAND 1551

The world will end in the year 1991.

DR. FREDERICK WM. HELLE — 1903

When the power of hell is let loose, seeds of evil will be swifter and the harvest of violence will be greater than was possible heretofore... More Apostasy can now be broadcast aided by inventions in five years, than was possible in prior centuries in fifty years.

ESSEN ELBERFELD — 1919

Even though Russia, Germany and Austria are now (1919) ripe for Antichrist, the socialist revolution (Communism) must seize the whole world before we can definitely take it for granted that his time has arrived.

BISHOP FULTON J. SHEEN — 1950

"The two great forces of the Mystical Body of Christ and the Mystical Body of the Antichrist are beginning to draw up their battle lines for the catastrophic combat. Communism is the Mystical Body of the Antichrist; its visible head is Stalin; its invisible head is the Devil; its members are not merely those who deny God, but those who challenge God, its Peter and Paul are Marx and Lenin; its Bible is Das Kapital; and its temporal city is the Kremlin.

"We are living the days of the Apocalypse — the last days of our era."

It could well be that Bishop Sheen is one of the Great Christian Preachers who will guide the Church during the last days as foretold in the Apocalypse.

THE NUMBER OF ELECT

Father Callistus, a confidante and spiritual director of the Blessed Anna Marie Taigi made the following statement from information given by her to him in about the year 1830: "The greater number of Christians today are damned." Anna Marie Taigi told me with her face clouded with an expression of infinite sadness:

"The destiny of those dying on one day is that very few — not as many as ten — went straight to heaven; many remained in purgatory; and those cast into hell were as numerous as flakes of snow in mid-winter." — Vie de la V. Anna Taigi, 5th Edition, p. 371

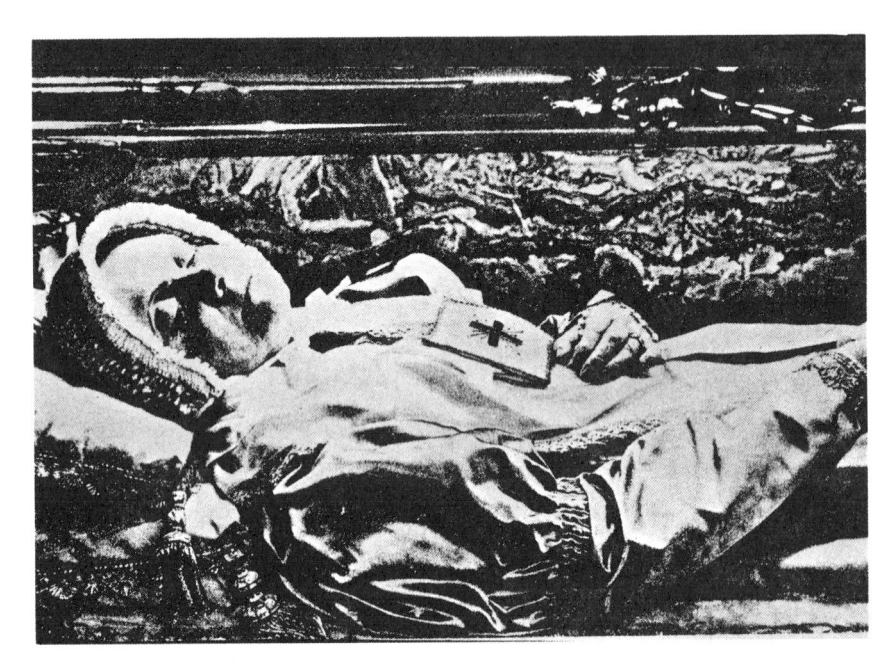

THE INCORRUPT BODY OF
BLESSED ANNA MARIE TAIGI

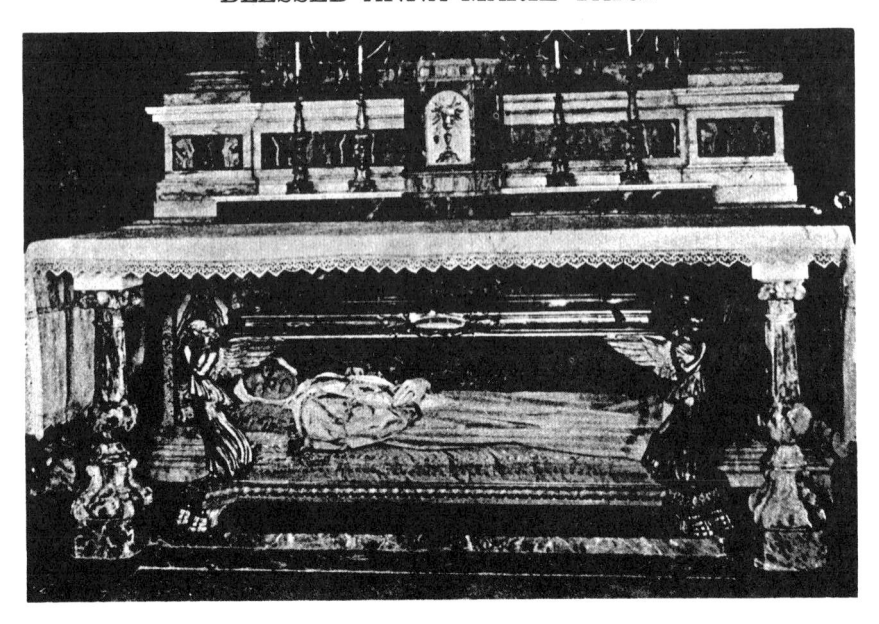

[134]

BLESSED ANNA MARIE TAIGI

A holy married woman will soon be canonized a saint. Popes and cardinals have referred to Blessed Anna Marie Taigi as one of the greatest saints of all time. She will be ranked among the great saints of the church. Our Blessed Mother appeared to her often and once said:

"In Anna Marie Taigi, we make known that housewives can be saints, and among the greatest of saints."

Pope Benedict, who beatified her on May 30, 1920, said "A humble wife and mother, an angel of consolation to her parents, a model for school girls and young women of the working class, a mother of children who knew how to unite labor with recollection, a mother of children upon whom weighed the care of her old parents, the care, too, of a husband who was not always good-tempered, and the education of a large family; a mother of children who, without neglecting any duty found time to visit the sick and to make herself all things to all men."

It was through her predictions of coming events that Mrs. Culligan and I became acquainted with this wonderful person. When we went to Rome for the first time we wanted to visit her resting place. We found her body, as shown on the opposite page, in perfect preservation after being dead over 100 years. On seeing this saint, Mrs. Culligan dropped on her knees beside her, where she remained for one-half hour. My Anna appeared to be in a trance. The two mothers, with seven children each, had much in common. Both were given the beautiful name of the mother of the Blessed Virgin — Anna Marie — and Anna Bridget. They are both saints. Housekeeping and the raising of their children always came before other religious duties. They both worshipped God on the altar of daily duty. The two mothers wore the large Carmelite brown scapulars. When their lives as housewives were finished, they devoted themselves exclusively to the worship of God. When Anna Bridget's youngest son went off to enter a Discalced Carmelite Seminary to study for the priesthood, and left our house on a California hilltop empty of children, she said to her husband: "Now my life's work is finished." He is now a priest.

A MIRACLE

After Anna Bridget arose from her trance-like experience kneeling before the body of Anna Marie Taigi, she said to me: "That was a most happy and tranquil experience." For many years, Anna Bridget had a severe physical ailment which left her while she knelt before Anna Marie. Her health became excellent, and has remained so for eight years. She never before knew such health. She was miraculously cured by Anna Marie Taigi without asking for it. Each mother understood the other's problems, and when it was possible for the one to help the other, she did so. It was a genuine miracle which took place that morning in Rome.

ANNA MARIE TAIGI PROPHESIES

God endowed Anna Marie Taigi with a vision that enabled her to see the secret of hearts and the coming of future events. She prophesied on the cataclysms which would precede the final triumph of the church. Her prophecies have been fulfilled with accuracy. She foretold the two world wars of this century. The one remaining unfulfilled prophecy is to occur towards the end of the world: "A punishment will be sent from Heaven" — of which she said: "There will come over all the earth intense darkness lasting three days and nights." While she lived, her humble home was visited daily by cardinals, bishops, princes and queens, who sought her counsel. This is Anna Marie's prophecy for our time:

"God will ordain two punishments; One, in the form of wars, revolutions and other evils, will originate on earth; the other will be sent from Heaven. There will come over all the earth an immense darkness lasting three days and three nights. Nothing will be visible and the air will be laden with pestilence, which will claim principally but not exclusively the enemies of religion. During this darkness artificial light will be impossible. Only blessed candles can be lighted and will afford illumination. He who out of curiosity opens his window to look out or leaves his house will fall dead on the spot. During these three days the people should remain in their homes, pray the Rosary and beg God for mercy. On this terrible occasion so many wicked men, enemies of His church, and of their God, shall be killed by this divine scourge. The enemies of the church, secret as well as known, will perish over the whole earth during that universal darkness. After the three days of darkness, Christianity will spread throughout the world. Whole nations will join the church shortly before the reign of Antichrist. These conversions will be amazing. Those who shall survive shall have to conduct themselves well. There shall be innumerable conversions of heretics. Russia, England and China will come into the church."

EARLY IRISH SAINTS FORETELL LAST DAYS
St. Malachy

We have the following words of St. Malachy — the archbishop of Armagh — one of the great Irish saints:

St. Malachy predicted, in 1130, "My beloved native Isle will undergo, at the hands of England, oppression, persecution, and calamities of every kind during ONE WEEK OF CENTURIES. But she will preserve her fidelity to God and to His church amidst all her trials." This prophecy was fulfilled to the letter. Ireland suffered terribly, to the start of the twentieth century. This suffering proved providential, and for a most important reason. Suffering, prayer and study makes for saints. Ireland has long been known as the home of "saints and scholars." For hundreds of years, no public Mass was permitted in Ireland. Of course, there were priests in hiding to say private and secret Mass. The Irish women recited rosaries almost constantly. This suffering of Irish people trained and prepared religious for foreign lands. For many hundreds of years, during the WEEK OF CENTURIES, as many as 12,000 religious — nuns and priests — left their homeland in Ireland yearly for the missions throughout the world, and are still doing so today in vast numbers. Think of it! Twelve-thousand religious per year from a population of about three million. In the State of California, with eighteen million population, we ordain less than one hundred priests per year. It takes hardship and suffering to produce our Catholic religious.

THE LAST WORLD WAR

"A GLIMPSE INTO HELL"
— *Courtesy The Harding Art Gallery, Chicago*

Our World is a great example of the axiom that experience teaches nothing. Just look at our times; our present PAGANISM, the multiplicity of our false teaching and the moral laxity that threaten to engulf us all in that devil sea of personal dishonesty, moral transgression, and international duplicity.
— FATHER MARTIN DEMPSEY

Chapter 13

Don't Risk Hell

All men on earth, who can never cease to be, will either spend eternity with Jesus Christ and His Father in heaven or be with the damned in hell forever. This is as certain as that the darkness of night follows the light of the day.

God is everywhere on earth and the knowledge of His existence is WRITTEN IN HEARTS OF ALL MEN. All souls while on earth, whatever may be their sins and their ignorance, move and live in His presence, and all are eligible for His mercy. He patiently awaits their turning to Him of their own free will when He will receive them; but He will not force them to love Him. He has said "Let no soul fear to come to Me even if its sin be as scarlet." This holds true until the moment of death after which GOD'S MERCY IS NO LONGER AVAILABLE. Hell is the withdrawal of His presence forever.

A book which is placed on the open market will naturally come into the hands of many readers, not all of whom share the same beliefs. The burden of this book is that mankind has been remiss in the obedience and service to God. If we have learned any lesson at all from history, it should be that just retribution is certain. This retribution is sometimes dealt to nations and individuals in time, but it is also true that those who die impenitent will find a punishment meted out to them in the judgment that is to come after death. God will consign the just to a place of everlasting happiness and the unjust to a place of everlasting torments. (Matt. 25:31-46.)

The recent Vatican Council II of the Catholic Church, respecting individual consciences, promulgated on December 7, 1965, the historic declaration on Religious Freedom. This consideration for the dignity of the human person, however, does not alter the belief of Catholics that truth is one, that God has revealed this truth and has founded one Church to promulgate it.

"First, the Council professes its belief that God Himself has made known to mankind the way in which men are to serve Him, and thus be saved in Christ and come to blessedness. We believe that this one true religion subsists in the Catholic and apostolic Church, to which the Lord Jesus committed the duty to spreading it abroad among all men. Thus He spoke to the Apostles: 'Go therefore and make disciples of all nations, baptizing them in the name of the Father and of the Son and of the Holy Spirit, teaching them to observe all things, whatsoever I have enjoined upon you.' (Matt. 28:19-20). On their part all men are bound to seek the truth, especially in what concerns God and His Church, and to embrace the truth they come to know, and to hold fast to it." (Declaration on Religious Freedom Par. 1)

For fifteen hundred years the unity of Christendom as regards doctrine remained intact — though schism separated one body of Christians from the other. But however well intentioned certain reformers in the sixteenth century brought about a disastrous division of Christendom into some 266 bodies, each holding somewhat different, and sometimes contradictory, beliefs.

This dissipation of the teachers and doctrines has resulted in the vast number of men calling into question the truths revealed to the Church. It is inconceivable that God would *will* such diversity, such confusion, such contradictions. It was Christ's prayer that "All would be one." Spurred on by the spectacle of Vatican Council II, and the ecumenical strides being made on all sides towards the reunion of Churches into THE Church, the time has come for all men seriously to consider the claims of the Catholic Church and to ponder the words of Holy Scripture: "They that believe not shall be condemned."

* * *

The contemplation of hell has made great saints, for we are told by Revelation that: "The fear of God is the beginning of wisdom." It is true to say that much holiness has been built on the fear of God and His judgment. When we contemplate the reality of hell we are building solidly for eternity. Hell is the expression of God's love. This may not be easily evident, but when we remember that God knows us in all our weakness as we can never know ourselves, perhaps we will come to understand, that for our own good, He will go very near to forcing us to love Him. "The fear of hell has to suffice when the love of God is not strong enough to gain our salvation."

BLESSED MOTHER WARNS

The Mother of Jesus has come to earth many times to save souls from the fires of hell. It is almost certain that there is no other reason for her visitations to La Salette, Lourdes and Fatima. At Fatima she left a prayer which she asked be repeated with every decade of the Rosary. The prayer is the key to all her visitations: "Oh, Jesus, forgive us our sins, *save us from the fires of hell,* lead all souls to heaven especially those most in need of Your mercy." On July 13, 1917, she opened up the earth so that the three shepherd children could look into hell. This was done so that the children could testify to the reality of this place of punishment for the wicked after death. The following is the description of this place of misery by the Fatima seers in Father Stephen Breen's book, "Recent apparitions of the Blessed Virgin Mary":

"The children saw emanating from her hands two bright and penetrating beams of light slanted obliquely to the surface of the earth, which seemed to penetrate the ground. A rift of some magnitude opened. Looking downward, the children saw a vision of hell. Down deep in the caverns of that frightful maelstrom, the three little seers gasped in horror at the dreadful spectacle. Lucia's gasp was audible: "Oh! Our Lady!" Lucia's account follows: "We saw a sea of fire in which were huge numbers of devils and damned souls in human form, plunged in deep immersions, all blackened and burnt, like transparent coals of black and bronze embers. They would be raised in the air by the flames, floating and swaying in clouds of flame and smoke, then falling back on all sides and in all directions, without weight or equilibrium and unable to control their movements. On fire within and without, they floated and showered about like sparks in a great conflagration amid shrieks and wailing screams of fiendish terror, pain and despair, which filled the fiery atmosphere. The sight caused her to shudder with horror and fear. We could tell the demons by their horrible, repugnant figures of loathsome and unknown animals which were blackened like coals by the fire, and yet were alive and transparent."

This hideous sight lasted only a minute for the children said they would die had it lasted longer. Our Lady looked on the children and said to them: "You have seen hell where the souls of poor sinners go. To save poor souls from hell God wishes to establish the devotion to my Immaculate Heart. If people do what I shall tell you MANY SOULS WILL BE SAVED."

Jacinta grew almost obsessed with the terrifying fate of souls damned through sin. "So many fall," she said. "So many fall."

"Hell . . . hell . . . " Jacinta repeated in an anguish of horror, "how they grieve me, those souls in hell . . . souls burning alive like wood in a fire . . ." Then she would fall upon her knees repeating the prayer Our Lady taught the three to say after each "Gloria" of the Rosary: "O my Jesus, forgive us our sins. Save us from the fires of hell, and lead all souls to Heaven, especially those in most need of Thy mercy."

"We must pray a great deal to save souls from hell," Jacinta would call out to her two companions, in the words of Our Lady, "Don't you want to prevent souls from falling into hell? So many souls go to hell!"

On one occasion Lucia reminded her of Our Lady's promise to take her to Heaven: "Do not be afraid; you are not going there; Our Lady is going to take you to Heaven with her."

"Yes, I know, *I want all those people and everybody to go there, too.* If only sinners could see hell and know what it is like, as we do, *they would not sin any more,* and no one would go to hell. Why didn't you ask Our Lady to show hell to all those people?"

SISTER JOSEFA MENENDEZ

Christ appeared often during the years 1921-22-23 to Sister Josefa Menendez — a coadjutrix sister of the Society of the Sacred Heart of Jesus. This Order is known in the United States as the Mesdames of the Sacred Heart.

The story of Christ's visits to Sister Josefa is a gripping and inspiring one. It is published in a book sponsored by the nun's own religious order — with instructions from Our Lord that

THE LAST WORLD WAR

its messages be broadcast widely. It contains over 500 pages, all of which are devoted to telling mankind how much Jesus Christ loves us, and begging all men and women to come to Him — with their love and receive Him.

In these pages Christ pleads with us to save our souls by finding His love before *"The approaching last days of the world."* This book is *The Way of Divine Love,* published by

SISTER JOSEFA MENENDEZ
Coadjutrix Sister
Of the Society of the Sacred Heart of Jesus
1890-1923

the Newman Press Westminster, Maryland, and by Sands & Company, London.

Our Lord sent Sister Josefa into hell so she, too, could testify to the torments of the damned to prepare men for heaven through the fear of God if "the love of God is not strong enough to gain us salvation." The following is Sister Josefa Menendez' own writing after her return from descents into hell.

Sister Josefa wrote with great reticence on the subject of hell. She did it only to conform to Our Blessed Lord's wishes, Our Lady having told her on the 25th October, 1922: "Everything that Jesus allows you to see and to suffer of the torments of hell, is . . . *that you may make it known.* So forget yourself entirely, and think only of the glory of the . . . *Salvation of souls.*

She repeatedly dwelt on the greatest torment of hell, namely:

"One of these damned souls cried out: 'This is my torture . . . that I want to love and cannot; there is nothing left me but hatred and despair. If one of us could so much as make a single act of love . . . this would no longer be hell. . . but we cannot, we live on hatred and malevolence . . .' (23rd March, 1922)."

Another of these unfortunates said: "The greatest of our torments here is that we are not able to love Him. While we hunger for love, we are consumed with desire of it, but it is too late."

She records, too, the accusations made against themselves by these unhappy souls: "Some yell because of the burning of their hands. Perhaps they were thieves, for they say: "Where is our loot now? . . . Cursed hands . . . Why did I want to possess what did not belong to me . . . and what in any case I could keep only for a few days?"

"Others curse their tongues, their eyes . . . whatever was the occasion of their sin . . . 'Now, O body, you are paying the price of the delights you granted yourself! . . . And you did it of your own free will . . .' " (2nd April 1922).

"I saw many worldly people fall into hell, and no words can render their horrible and terrifying cries: 'Damned for ever . . . I deceived myself; I am lost . . . I am here for ever'."

"Today, I saw a vast number of people fall into the fiery pit

... they seemed to be worldlings and a demon cried vociferously: 'The world is ripe for me . . . I know that the best way to get hold of souls is to rouse their desire for enjoyment . . . Put *me* first . . . *Me* before the rest . . . no humility for *me!* But let me enjoy myself . . . This sort of thing assures victory to me . . . and they tumble headlong into hell'." (4th October 1922).

"Tonight," wrote Josefa, "I did not go down into hell, but was transported to a place where all was obscure, but in the center was a red smouldering fire. They had laid me flat and so bound me that I could not make the slightest movement. Around me were seven or eight people; their black bodies were unclothed, and I could see them only by the reflections of the fire. They were seated and were talking together.

"One devil to another said: 'We'll have to be very careful not to be found out, for we might easily be discovered.'

"Another devil answered: 'Insinuate yourselves by including carelessness in them . . . but keep in the background, so that you are not found out . . . by degrees they will become callous, and you will be able to incline them to evil. Tempt these others to ambition, to self-interest, TO ACQUIRING WEALTH WITHOUT WORKING . . . Excite some to sensuality and love of pleasure'."

Josefa, on her return from hell, noted the following: "I saw several souls fall into hell, and among them was a child of fifteen, cursing her parents for not having taught her to fear God nor that there was a hell. Her life had been a short one, she said, but full of sin, for she had given in to all that her body and passions demanded in the way of satisfaction. *Especially she had read bad books*." (22nd March, 1923).

"Sounds of confusion and blasphemy cease not for an instant. A sickening stench asphyxiates and corrupts everything; it is like the burning of putrefied flesh, mingled with tar and sulphur . . . a mixture to which nothing on earth can be compared."

ST. TERESA, TOO, WAS SHOWN HELL

St. Teresa, 1515-1582, was given a vision of HELL. She said of this experience:

"The humble man never forgets that Christ has delivered him from the fires of Hell."

One of the most unforgetable experiences in St. Teresa's life was her famous vision of HELL which she considered a "most signal favor" from God. She beheld souls tormented by fire and despair, saw the place the devils had prepared for her because of her sins, and realized most vividly that only God's mercy had delivered her from such terrible and enduring torments (Life, Chapter XXXII). This vision of HELL was one of the significant events in St. Teresa's life that led ultimately to the foundation of the Carmelite Reform; but it also influenced her to thoughts of humility. Her words on humility are often related to HELL.

THIS CHAPTER AIMS AT SAVING SOULS

This is my most important chapter. The aim of the book — the reason for its being written is: TO SAVE SOULS. There are two fine American paintings on HELL. I was able to have colored plates made from them for printing in this chapter. HELL is Satan's eternal home. It has been his home since his banishment from Heaven, for his sins of pride. His aim ever since has been to induce creatures of earth to join him in HELL.

Satan has convinced many people of earth that there is no HELL. To this I answer: "The Hell there's not!'" It is the author's hope that if words will not convince some Americans that they should NOT RISK HELL, that these paintings will do so; that the torments suffered by the damned may prepare people for Heaven through fear of God, if their love for Him is not strong enough to gain their salvation.

I appeal to the readers of this little volume not to risk the fires of hell. They are real. They are intense. They are eternal.

A decree issued by the Holy See in 1890 forbids priests to give sacramental absolution to those who deny the reality of the fire of hell.

The view that time would bring a mitigation of the pains of hell was condemned by the Congregation of the Holy Office in 1893.

(Matt. 17:26.) "How is a man the better for it if he gains the whole world at the cost of losing his own soul."

If there was no hell from which to save us, why did Christ die on the cross?

OUR LADY OF THE ROSARY
The Culligan Family Shrine

Part Five

Mary Our Hope

Chapter 14

Mary Our Hope

It is through the most Blessed Virgin Mary that Jesus Christ has come into the world and it is also through her that He ought to reign in the world . . . In these last times the Blessed Virgin will be better known and revealed by the Holy Ghost in order to make Jesus Christ better known, loved, and served. . . In these last times, Mary must show forth more than ever her mercy, to bring back and lovingly receive poor sinners who will be converted, and her strength against the enemies of God, wicked and hardened, who will cause terrible revolutions and seduce many by their promises and threats! . . . Mary will be terrible to the devil and his followers, like an army set in battle array. — SAINT LOUIS GRIGNON DE MONTFORT writing in *True Devotion* in the 18th century.

It is impossible to consider the numerous apparitions of the Mother of God upon earth, especially since 1830, apart from their relation to world events. It is not to say anything new to say that we find ourselves today a rudderless ship at sea, being tossed to and fro by the winds and waves, unable to chart our course or to find our way. No derelict ship, no ship without a pilot, ever found its way into port. On the contrary, every such vessel on the high sea is not only a loss itself but is also a menace to others. The ocean's floor is strewn with old Spanish galleons and Roman turiremes that did not find their way into port, and there are those fearfully watching our floundering ship who say that ere long we are likely to take our place among them.

Actually I do not think we are without a pilot. Our Blessed Mother has offered to take her place at the helm and has given us very clear instructions as to how we are to ride the storm and come successfully into port.

THE LAST WORLD WAR

THE APOCALYPSE

Many Marian writers are of the opinion that the Apocalypse started in the chapel shown here.

The chapel is that of the Sisters of St. Vincent de Paul, Rue du Bac, Paris, where Our Blessed Mother appeared to St. Catherine in 1830. The statue above the right side altar and shown to the right is as the Virgin first appeared to St. Catherine. The remains of the saint are in perfect state of preservation. In this same chapel Our Lady appeared also to Sister Bisqueburu in 1840 to give the green scapular to the world.

[152]

As I hear the maternal warnings, I do not always find the punishing hand of an angry Father raised to strike, but I do hear the solicitous words of a loving Mother telling us that if the Father cannot guide us gently home, He may have to resort to more drastic measures, not because He wants to punish us, but because we are wilful and wayward children and cannot understand or will not heed the softer language of love.

Man is by nature a philosopher. He is a rational creature, always seeking the ultimate causes of things. On a purely natural level he can sometimes succeed very well, but when it comes to understanding the factors or work in the supernatural order of grace, man is often bewildered. For instance, it is hard to understand why a young mother is sometimes snatched by death, leaving a brood of small children without a mother's care, while an unmarried and childless woman lives on to enjoy many years of unfettered liberty. There are many such riddles in the world of grace which man's unaided reason cannot solve. That is what Revelation is for.

One of the most common of these riddles is the restlessness of human nature and its dissatisfaction with all earthly things. Men strive for one thing after another, and when the object is attained, they are not content; they must have more. Now Holy Scripture interprets this restlessness for us, this unceasing dissatisfaction with what has been acquired. It tells us that a man was made for God. On every page of the Bible this fact is repeated: man cannot get along without God.

Scripture opens with a picture of man in the peace and joy of life near to God; then sin enters and disturbs this close relationship, which was the secret of all his happiness. The gates of Eden are closed upon man in rebellion against God.

Scripture closes with man restored to his peace in the vision of God. The highest hope that revelation inspires is this: that sinful man can return to God. This is the Gospel; the glad tidings of great joy. Between these two pictures of happiness forfeited and happiness restored, is the history of a long, wild, passionate struggle, now in one way, now in another, to get back that happiness which man felt he ought to have; and in the midst of this endless struggle, God is seen striving to make Himself known and heard, sending blessings and successes and, when necessary, failure, suffering, and dissatisfaction, and calling to him "O man, thou wert made for God, and thy heart is restless till it find its rest in Him."

Like the Good Shepherd that He is, God hears the bleating of His sheep on the moor, in danger of wolves and destruction. In times past He has sent out His call to avert the disasters of history, to warn us. Since 1830, first at the Motherhouse of the Sisters of Charity in Paris, then at La Salette, 1846, at Knock and Lourdes and Pontmain and at Fatima in 1917, the Mother of God was permitted to speak to us through her apparitions. Two of these are especially useful in our study here and I am narrating at some length the great message of La Salette, and with less space the warning at Fatima.

In the dark days of post-revolutionary France, when the Church's eldest daughter had turned rationalistic, liberalistic, and religiously indifferent, a priest, Father William Joseph Chaminade, took up his pen and wrote these words of encouragement to his spiritual children:[1]

"All periods of the Church's history are marked with the struggles and the triumphs of the august Mary. Ever since the Lord put enmity between her and the serpent, she has constantly overcome the world and hell. All the heresies, the Church tells us, have been vanquished by the Blessed Virgin, and little by little she has reduced them to the silence of death.

"In our day the prevailing great heresy is religious indifference which is casting on souls the deadly sleep of selfishness and the blight of passion. The depths of the infernal abyss vomit forth dense clouds of black and pestilential smoke that threatens to envelop the whole earth in a dark night, void of good, full of all evil, and impenetrable, we might say, to the life-giving rays of the Sun of Justice. Consequently the divine light of faith is growing dim and being extinguished in the very midst of the Christian world; virtue is becoming more and more rare, is disappearing, whilst vice is breaking loose with frightful fury. It seems that we are about to see what has been foretold, a general defection and an apostasy really all but universal.

"This description of our times, unfortunately so exact, is,

---

[1] Quoted by George Montague, S.M., in *Mary's War Against Communism*, St. Meinrad, Ind., p. 1-2.

however, far from discouraging us. Mary's power is not diminished. We firmly believe that she will overcome this heresy as she has overcome all others, because she is today, as she was formerly, the incomparable Woman, the promised Woman, who was to crush the serpent's head . . . To her, therefore, is reserved a great victory in our day; hers will be the glory of saving the faith from the shipwreck with which it is threatened among us."

When the first news came to America of Our Lady's Fatima visitation, people were spell-bound with the wonderment of a message direct from heaven to guide men and women on earth. But such a message was not new. The Fatima message has since become so well known, no doubt, because it carried a promise of peace for a world filled with the fear of war. There have been previous public visitations of Our Blessed Mother which are just as important as the Fatima visit, but which are not so well known because unlike Fatima, some of them condemned man severely for his sinful ways. We will outline here a few of the many public visitations and give the main purpose of each visit.

When Our Blessed Mother appeared at Knock, County Mayo, Ireland, on August 21, 1879, St. John accompanied her with a book in his hand. Students of the "Last Days" believe that when the author of the Apocalypse was seen with Mary this may indicate that the events foretold in the Apocalypse were to start as of then. Seventy years later, this visit of Mary, St. Joseph and St. John to earth seems to be the beginning of the fulfillment of the last events of the Bible, and explains the reason for the many other revelations and appearances for the past 135 years. She came for many reasons, among them being to interpret the little understood passages of the Apocalypse, and thus prepare her children for her Son's second Coming.

"Mary, herself, is a sign of modern times, the greatest sign, just as John the Baptist was the greatest sign of his time. She came to herald the new coming of her son as the Baptist had come to herald His first coming to earth through her. She said at La Salette and Lourdes, in effect, exactly what John had said of the coming of Christ, and she was to say it most dramatically at Fatima when the evil of the last century was yielding its first fruits of world war."[1]

---

[1] *Recent Apparitions of the Blessed Virgin Mary.* — STEPHEN BREEN

THE LAST WORLD WAR

The underlying purpose of the many visits of the Queen of Heaven to earth was to gain souls for the final gigantic struggle between "Her sign and the Star of the Abyss." The struggle started in the Garden of Eden. This same enmity between Satan and "The Woman" is now dividing the members of Christ's Mystical Body, and the members of the Diabolical Mystical Body of Satan.

All messages since 1830 to Sister Catherine Laboure read like a continued story and could well be considered one message, for all follow the same theme — Pray, Pray, Pray, and do penance. These messages warned of punishment that would fall on a sinful world, and they have come as foretold. Each message, however, had a special purpose of great significance. Her apparitions are special interventions of Divine Providence to urge the faithful to penance and prayer and to lead wayward souls to His mercy while there is still time. Christ said at Heede (Germany) in 1938: "Before I come as the Just One, I first open wide the gates of mercy. Let no soul fear to come to me even if its sins be as scarlet. While there is still time let them take refuge in the font of My mercy."

The Mother of Jesus promised peace to the world — for a time — on October 13, 1917, at Fatima, Portugal, if we amend our lives and say the Rosary. If we did not do as she asked, she foretold there would be a more terrible war. These are her words to three children:

"You have seen Hell, where the souls of poor sinners go. To save them, God wishes to establish throughout the world devotion to My Immaculate Heart. If people do what I tell you, many souls will be saved, and there will be Peace.

"But, if they do not stop offending God, another and more terrible war will break out in the reign of Pius XI. When a night ILLUMINED BY AN UNKNOWN LIGHT is seen, know that this is the signal that God gives that the chastisement of the world for its many transgressions is at hand." The unknown light in question was seen all over Europe and North America, the night of January 24-25, 1938. It was an ominous red glow, as if great cities were on fire. Three months later, Hitler invaded Austria. The 'chastisement of the world' was about to become a terrible reality, the most terrible reality (to date) mankind has ever known.

LIGHT DESCRIBED
The New York Times' Account

The New York Times for January 26, 1938, carried the following:

"London, January 25th, 1938. The Aurora Borealis rarely seen in Southern or Western Europe spread fear in parts of Portugal and lower Austria tonight while thousands of Britons were brought running into the streets in wonderment. The ruddy glow led many to think half the city was ablaze. The Windsor Fire Department was called out thinking that Windsor Castle was afire. The lights were clearly seen in Italy, Spain, and even Gibraltar. The glow bathing snow-clad mountain tops in Austria and Switzerland was a beautiful sight but firemen turned out to chase non-existent fires. Portuguese villagers rushed in fright from their homes fearing the end of the world."

"Grenoble, France, January 25th, 1938. A huge blood-red beam of light which scientists said was an Aurora Borealis of exceptional amplitude tied up telephone systems in parts of France tonight and spread anxiety in numerous Swiss Alpine villages. Emblazoned in the Northern sky the light brought thousands of telephone calls to Swiss and French authorities asking whether it was a Fire? War? or the End of the World?"

THE LITERARY DIGEST ACCOUNT

"Thousands of frightened Portuguese peasants rushed from their homes one night recently and pointed to huge shafts of blood-red, greenish-blue and purple light shimmering on the northern horizon. 'It's the end of the world!' they cried.

"In London the luminous heavens also caused alarm. Half the city appeared to be ablaze. Frantic citizens telephoned newspaper offices. 'Where's the fire?' they asked. Out in Windsor fire engines clanged through the streets. 'Windsor Castle is afire,' everyone said.

"In southwestern France, in the Alpine villages of Switzerland and along the Danube in Austria, the heavenly blaze brought thousands into city streets and country roads. 'Fire?' they asked one another. 'War?' 'Doomsday?'

"In Holland crowds awaiting the birth of Crown Princess Juliana's baby hailed the celestial spectacle. 'A good omen,' they said. But in the lowlands of Scotland, men and women shook their heads. 'Northern lights,' they declared, 'always spell misfortune for Scotland.'

"The excitement spread across the Atlantic. Bermudians stared at the distant glow. In Canada, much closer to the phenomenon, the Canadian Press reported that 'wire services throughout northern Ontario were disrupted,' while radio transmission went dead."

The following week *Literary Digest* (February 19, 1938) in the featured news picture on page 1 showed a conference of Hitler, Goebbels and Goering, with the following caption:

"Fuehrer Takes All: In a sudden, secret, bloodless purge, Adolph Hitler has re-organized army, air force, diplomatic corps and cabinet. Whether or not Hitler's sweeping changes presaged a change in foreign policy remained a matter of speculation last week."

"Hitler entered Austria on March 11, 1938 and on March 13, Austria was declared a part of the German Reich. This was the first move in World War II. The lights referred to above appeared on the night of January 24-25, 1938. The move upon Austria took place 45 to 48 days later."

OUR LADY OF FATIMA

The six visitations of Our Blessed Mother to Fatima, Portugal, at noon on the 13th day of the months of May, June, July, (August[1]), September and October in the year 1917 are well known to Catholic people. For the benefit of non-Catholics who may not be familiar with them, allow me a brief description.

The Blessed Mother appeared to three shepherd children in a field where they attended sheep. The oldest was Lucy dos Santos, age nine, and her cousins, Francisco and Jacinta Marto, ages eight and six. At noon on May 13, 1917, as these children were looking toward a small oak tree a dazzling light hovered

---

[1]Because of the detention of the children by the Mayor of Ourem, no apparition occurred on August 13, though the people gathered in the Cova, did see and hear phenomena associated with the other apparitions.

over it, and in this light was a lovely Lady. She was like an angel — "She was a Lady more brilliant than the sun," said Lucy. She appeared over this tree five times, always at noontime. During these visits to these children she left with them the now well known Fatima messages promising peace if men amended their lives, and terrible punishment if men did not heed her warning.

"I come to ask the consecration of Russia to My Immaculate Heart and the Communion of Reparation on the first Saturdays. If people heed my request, Russia will be converted and there will be Peace. If not, she will spread her errors throughout the world, promoting wars and persecution of the Church. The good will be martyred; the Holy Father will suffer much; different nations will be destroyed, but in the end My Immaculate Heart will triumph. The Holy Father will consecrate Russia to me, which will be converted and some time of peace will be given to the world."

She promised a miracle on her last appearance to convince the world that her visits were from heaven. This miracle had to do with solar activity. The following is a description of what happened on October 13, 1917.

Gradually the sun grew pale, lost its normal color and appeared as a sort of silver disc at which all could gaze directly without even shading their eyes. Then, to the astonishment of all present, rays of multicolored light shot out from the sun in every direction; red, blue, green, yellow — every color of the spectrum. Meanwhile, the whole heavens seemed to be revolving as the sun spun madly on its axis like a gigantic wheel of fire, painting the rocks, the trees, the faces of the people with sunshine, such as human eye had never seen before. Three times it stopped and three times the mad dance was resumed. Then, while the crowd fell to its knees in sheer terror, the sun suddenly seemed to be torn loose from its place in the heavens. Down it hurtled, closer and closer to earth, staggering "drunkenly" as it zig-zagged through the skies while from all parts of the now thoroughly terrified multitude arose cries of repentance and appeals for mercy. "It's the end of the world!" shrieked one woman hysterically. "Dear God, don't let me die in my sins!" implored another. But just when it seemed that the end was at hand, the sun suddenly resumed its accustomed place in the heavens, whence it shone forth as peacefully as before.

WHAT HAS HAPPENED TO HEEDE?

In the early fifties, as many of our readers will remember, reports of a series of apparitions of Our Lord and Our Lady at Heede, a small village in northern Germany were current.[1]

It was alleged that more than one hundred apparitions took place, and that prudent priests sent by the Bishop to investigate the happenings had made a favourable report.

Some of the statements made by Our Lord and His Blessed Mother are of profound interest to the modern world.

When four girls reported, on November 1, 1937, that the Blessed Virgin had appeared to them, the news was received in the village with predictable scepticism and/or amusement.

It was not until the girls showed a dramatic change in their way of life that the villagers began to wonder. Hitherto given over to pleasures and amusements, the girls switched to long and fervent prayer, impatiently waiting for the hour when they would see the Heavenly Vision again.

Nevertheless, the Pastor and most of the villagers refused to believe in the apparitions for a long time but were finally won over.

Crowds came to Heede when the news percolated to the surrounding towns and villages. But Hitler ruled Germany in those days, and the Gestapo swiftly put a stop to this "superstitious nonsense."

The children were taken to an asylum and the pilgrimages forbidden. After a few weeks the children were released, but forbidden to go near the place of the Apparitions. However Our Lady appeared to them in other places, as subsequently did Our Lord.

The Message

The message of Heede is very similar to that of Fatima.

Our Lady appears to have said little. She appeared to the girls with the Divine Child in her arms, smiled at them and was content to have them enraptured with the beauty of the Divine presence.

---

[1] North American Voice of Fatima

She did however ask for prayer and penance, particularly the Rosary, and that she be named Queen of the Universe.

When Our Lord — as a grown man — appeared to one of the seers, Greta Gansforth, He had a solemn and sad warning to give her.

"Men did not listen to My Most Holy Mother when She appeared to them at Fatima and admonished them to do penance. Now I Myself am coming at the last hour to warn and admonish mankind! The times are very serious! Men should at last do penance, turn away from their sins and pray, pray much in order that the wrath of God may be mitigated! Particularly the Holy Rosary should be prayed very often! The Rosary is very powerful with God! Worldly pleasures and amusements should be restricted.

"Men do not listen to My voice, they harden their hearts, they resist My grace, they do not wish to have anything to do with My Mercy, My Love, My merits; mankind is worse than before the deluge. Mankind is suffocating in sin. Hatred and greed rule their hearts. This is the work of the Devil. They live in great darkness . . .

"Through the wounds that bleed now, mercy will again gain victory over justice. My faithful souls should not be asleep now like the disciples on Mt. Olivet. They should pray without ceasing and gain all they can for themselves and for others.

"Tremendous things are in preparation; it will be terrible as never before since the foundation of the world. All those who in these grave times have suffered so much, are martyrs and form the seed for the new Church. They were privileged to participate in My captivity, in My scourging, in My crown of thorns, and My way of the Cross!

"The Blessed Virgin Mary and all the choirs of Angels will be active during the happenings. Hell believes that it is sure of the harvest, but I will snatch it away from them. Many curse Me now, but these sufferings will come over mankind that they may be saved through it . . . Many expiate all they can for those who curse Me now.

"I will come with My peace. With a few faithful, I will build up My Kingdom. As a flash of lightning this Kingdom will come . . . much faster than mankind will realize. I will give them a special light. For some this light will be a blessing; for others, darkness. The light will come like the Star that showed the way to the wise men. Mankind will experience My love and My power. I will show them My justice and My mercy.

"My dearly beloved children, the hour comes closer and closer. Pray without ceasing!"

APPARITION ON MAY 26, 1946[1]

"Yes, I am the powerful Mediatrix of Grace. As the world can find mercy only through the sacrifice of the Son with the Father, so can you only find favor with the Son through my intercession. Christ is too unknown, because I am not known. Because the nations rejected His Son, the Father poured out His cup of wrath upon them. It is true that the world was consecrated to My Immaculate Heart, but this consecration has become a fearful responsibility for many men. I demand that the world live this consecration. Have unreserved confidence in My Immaculate Heart! Believe that I am able to do everything with My Son. Substitute My Immaculate Heart in place of your sinful hearts. Then, it will be I who will draw the power of God and the love of the Father will renew the fullness of Christ in you. Fulfill my request so that Christ may reign as the King of Peace.

"After this, the devil will be possessed of such power that those who are not firmly established in Me will be deceived. There is a time coming when you will stand in this place all alone and be frightfully calumniated. The devil knows how to deceive men so that they permit themselves to be completely blinded to the higher things. The devil has power over all people who do not trust in My heart. Wherever people substitute My Immaculate Heart for their sinful hearts, the devil has no power. But he will persecute My children. They will be despised, but he can do them no harm."

APPARITION, JUNE 25, 1946

"I am the POWERFUL MEDIATRIX OF GRACE. It is the

---

[1] The report of the Apparition of the Mother of God in Marienfried near Pfaffenhofen on the road near Neuulm, Germany. By Rev. Father Martin Rumph, Pastor.

will of the Father that the world acknowledge this position of His Handmaid. People must believe that I am the permanent Bride of the Holy Ghost, and the faithful Mediatrix of all graces. My SIGN is already appearing. God wants it so. Only my children recognize this Sign because it reveals itself in secret, and for it they give glory to the Eternal God. I cannot manifest my power to the world in general. I must still hold myself aloof with my children. In secret I shall work marvels in souls till the required number of victims will be filled. Upon you it depends to shorten the days of darkness. Your blood and your sacrifices shall destroy the image of the beast. Then, I can manifest myself to the world for the glory of the Almighty. Choose my Sign, so that the Triune God may soon be adored and honored. Pray and offer sacrifices through me. Pray always; pray the Rosary. Make all your entreaties to the Father through My Immaculate Heart. If they are conducive to His Honor, He will grant them. . . . I urge my people to fulfill my wishes quickly because today, and ever, such fulfillment of my will, is necessary for God's greater honor and glory. The Father pronounces a dreadful woe upon all who refuse to obey His Will.

"The world will have to drain the cup of wrath to the dregs because of the countless sins through which His heart is offended. The star of the internal regions will rage more violently than ever and will cause frightful destruction, because he knows that his time is short, and because he sees that already many have gathered around my sign. Over these he has no power, although he will kill the bodies of many; but through these sacrifices brought for me, my power to lead the remaining host to victory will increase. Some have already allowed my sign to be impressed on them; their number will keep growing. But, I want to tell you, my children, not to forget that the very cross of those bloody days is a grace. Pray, make sacrifices for sinners. Offer yourselves and your works to the Father through me, and put yourself at my disposal without reserve. Pray the Rosary. Pray not so much for external things — weightier things are at stake in these times. Expect no sign or wonders. I shall be active as the powerful Mediatrix in secret. For you I shall procure peace of heart, if you will fulfill this request. . . ."

(The following is an extract taken from the September, 1948, issue of the "Christian Family Magazine," published by the Fathers of the Society of the Divine Word, Techny, Illinois.)

"The importance of the revelation of Pfaffenhofen can hardly be exaggerated. It is a strong confirmation of Fatima. There, Mary demanded, and Pope Pius XII carried out, the world dedications to her Immaculate Heart. Mary said 'that this dedication for many has become a terrible responsibility.' Mary wishes that 'this dedication be lived,' that hence the message of Fatima be treated most seriously. At the same time, she announced that God's punishments are very close, that a gigantic struggle between her 'Sign' and the 'Star of the Abyss' is at hand. Thus, the revelations enter the ultimate world perspectives. The Holy Virgin Mother cannot admonish the world enough to cling to her and through her to Christ. Only thus can mankind conquer in the approaching battle."

* * *

On reading the foregoing, one will realize that Our Blessed Mother's plan, behind Her visits to earth, is to prepare people for the coming of Antichrist, so that they will be fortified, through prayer, to have the courage in their own personal battle against the beast. This is borne out in the prayer She has asked us to say after each decade of our Rosary:

"Jesus, forgive us our sins, and save us from the fires of Hell . . . O My Jesus."

OUR LADY OF LA SALETTE

Any mother who watches her son die knows agony. But none has ever known the agony Mary Immaculate endured as she watched the loveliest of all Sons die on a cross. Yet, had that sacrifice been accepted by men as it was by God, had all the sons of Adam acknowledged Jesus as Savior and adored Him as God, Mary could have borne her agony with even greater dignity. But what are the facts? Over 1800 years after His death, she was still weeping — and with reason! In 1846 there were over one billion 500 million inhabitants on the earth, but only an infinitesimal fraction of them had really fallen in love with Mary's Son.

When Our Lady appeared at La Salette (France) she was more typically herself than at any of her public apparitions. As her Son's suffering overflowed in blood, her sufferings overflowed in tears. Jesus and His Mother both came into their glory through suffering. Suffering will continue within His Mystical Body as long as there is sin on earth. All of us living within His Body must suffer as the blood of Christ flows through us. Worldly people often ask: Why does God permit such a good person to suffer? The true friends of God very often must bear great suffering. By doing so they make up what is missing in His Passion. The poorest on this earth are nearest to Our Lord. Those within the diabolical mystical body of Satan are often free of all suffering, living in ease, with worldly adornments and wealth. Satan promises great material possessions and a life of physical pleasure to those who give up Christ and "sell out" to him, and he often keeps his promise. The modern materialistic world is Satan's kingdom, and money is the God he gives his people to worship. As materialism, atheism and the cruelty in human society constantly increase, so Christ's Mystical Body must suffer in greater volume. But this cannot go on forever. We would be unable to bear suffering in ever increasing amounts. Christ said it will end. This writer believes it is destined to end in our time. He believes present world-wide Godlessness will soon bring on the death of the Mystical Body as it formerly brought death to His human body; that Christ's church will go into hiding in its sepulchre until another resurrection. He believes on that glorious Easter morning will start the Peace promised by Mary at Fatima, which will bring on the dawn of infinite Peace. It will be the day which we have awaited for thousands of years. In the meantime, there will be more and greater suffering.

The suffering of Our Sorrowful Mother is the explanation why so many Catholics have been poor, sick and heavily-laden. Our kingdom has not been of this world. This world for us has been but a short novitiate.

But God is just as well as merciful. Had not the time come for justice? Mary, being Mother of Man as well as Mother of God, would do what she could for both. She implored Him to withhold His just anger — and appeared on the mountain of

OUR SORROWFUL MOTHER

at La Salette

La Salette, weeping and warning men. She cried: "I am no longer able to restrain the arm of my son."

In tears she appeared to two children and told them the cause of her grief, instructing them to tell part of her message at once, and the full message in 12 years. Popes Pius IX and Leo XIII heard these messages and believed them. However, to this day the greater part of her La Salette message is not well known. After 100 years it still is fearsome reading. It tells the wrath of God for a sinful world in words which cannot be misunderstood. It is my belief our Blessed Mother succeeded in delaying punishment for 54 years.

We all know that the world has fallen into greater wickedness during these years of grace with the race perverting itself more and more as it grows older. It would seem that God's plan for repopulating Heaven by creating earth, and then man and woman to live on it, giving them free will to choose between His Father and Satan, was meeting with poor success.

This writer is of the opinion that all people should study both the Messages of La Salette and the Messages of Fatima side by side, and consider them as one with one message complementing and interpreting the other. On reading the two messages we begin to understand the Plan God has for the punishment of the world.

The Fatima Messages have been widely distributed because they carry hope for peace, but the La Salette Message was not, because, no doubt, it carries no hope for peace and warns of impending doom. In any event, it is certain that the Blessed Mother wanted the people of the world to be guided by the La Salette Messages as well as the Fatima Messages. She did not want the La Salette Message kept a secret beyond the year 1858.

THE MESSAGE OF LA SALETTE

The public message of La Salette is available and is well known. I wish only to publish here the secret messages of both children which were given to Pope Pius IX.

The La Salette apparition preceded the Lourdes apparition to St. Bernadette by 12 years. The Blessed Virgin appeared on the now famous La Salette Mount in France to two children.

One was a little shepherd boy, 11 years of age, and the other a poor, timid girl, 14 years of age. These two children suddenly became famous in France, Italy, and throughout Europe. The name of the boy is: Peter Maximin Giraud; and that of the girl: Frances Melanie Mathieu. On Saturday, September 19, 1846, between 2 and 3 o'clock in the afternoon, they both beheld the apparition recognized as worthy of credence by Pope Pius IX on August 24, 1852, and has since been known throughout the Catholic world as Our Lady of La Salette. The following are the secret messages:[1]

SECRET OF MAXIMIN GIRAUD

"On the 19th of September, 1846, I saw a lady brilliant like the sun, whom I believe to be the Holy Virgin. However, I have never said it was the Holy Virgin. I have always said that I saw a lady, but never ventured to affirm that it was the Holy Virgin.

"From what I am going to state here, it appertains to the Church to judge whether it was truly the Holy Virgin or some other person. She gave me my secret about the middle of her conversation with me, after these words: 'The grapes shall rot, and the chestnuts shall be bad.' The Lady began by saying to me:

"1. 'Three fourths of France shall lose the faith, and the other fourth, that will preserve it, will practice it with tepidity.

"2. 'Peace shall not be given to the world until men will be converted.

"3. 'A Protestant nation in the North shall be converted to the faith, and through the means of that nation, the others shall return to the holy Catholic Church.

"4. 'The next Pope shall not be a Roman.

"5. 'When men shall be converted, God will give peace to the world.

"6. 'Afterwards this peace shall be disturbed by the monster.

---

[1] From "Christian Trumpet," by Pellegrino. Publisher, Patrick Donahoe, Boston, 1878, "La Vie de Melanie," Leon Bloye, 1915, and from "The Reign of Antichrist," by Cullerton, Fresno, Calif., 1951.

"7. 'The monster shall arrive at the end of this nineteenth century or, at latest, at the commencement of the twentieth.

"8. 'In this time the Antichrist will be born of a nun of Hebraic descent, a false virgin, who will have intercourse with the ancient serpent, with the master of impurity and putrefaction. His father will be a bishop. He will perform false miracles and subsist only on vitiating faith. He will have his brethren, who will be children of evil but not incarnate devils like himself. Soon they will be at the head of armies, supported by the legions of hell.

"9. 'Up, ye children of light, and fight! For behold, the age of ages, the end, the extremity is at hand! The Church passes into darkness. The world will be in a state of consternation, perplexity and confusion.

"10. On Henoch and Elias: 'They will suddenly appear on earth full of the spirit of God, when the Church becomes darkened and the world in terrible agony. They will convert those of good will and comfort the oppressed Christians. With the help of the Holy Ghost, they will have great success against the heresies of the Antichrist. But in the end they will be delivered unto death'."

SECRET OF MELANIE MATHIEU

Melanie's secret message, which follows, was published in its entirety in a brochure which she had printed in 1879 at Lecce, Italy, with the approval of the Bishop of Lecce.

"The Lady said to me:

" 'What I shall tell you now will not always remain a secret. You are allowed to publish it after the year 1858.

" 'There will be a kind of false peace before the advent of Antichrist. Man's only thought will be upon diversions and amusements. The wicked will indulge in all sorts of sin, but the children of the Holy Church, the children of the faith, my sincere followers, will wax strong in the love of God and in the virtues that are dear to me. Happy the humble souls that are guided by the Holy Ghost. I will fight with them until they shall have reached the completion of age.

" 'Italy will be severely punished for her efforts to shake off the yoke of the Most High Lord. She will become the play-ball of war. On every side blood will flow. The temples will either be closed or desecrated. Priests and members of religious orders will be put to flight. They will be beaten to death and otherwise die cruel deaths.

" 'The Vicar of My Son will be compelled to suffer much because for a time the Church will be delivered to great persecutions. That will be the hour of darkness, and the Church will experience a frightful crisis. The powerful officials of the State and the Church will be suppressed and done away with, and all law and order as well as justice. There will be murder, hate, envy and deceit, with no love or regard for one's country or family.

" 'God is going to punish in a manner without example. Woe to the inhabitants of the earth! God is going to exhaust His wrath, and nobody shall be able to evade so many combined evils. At the first stroke of His fulminating sword the mountains and the whole of nature shall shake with terror, because the disorders and crimes of men pierce the very vaults of the heavens. The earth shall be stricken with every kind of plagues. (Besides the pestilence and famine, which shall be general.) There shall be wars until the last war, which shall be waged by the ten kings of Antichrist. All these kings shall have a common design, and they only shall govern the world. Priests and religious shall be hunted; they shall be butchered in a cruel manner. Many shall abandon the faith, and great shall be the number of priests and religious who shall separate themselves from the true religion; among these there will be found likewise several bishops. Let the Pope be upon his guard against miracle-workers, for the time is arrived when the most astounding prodigies will take place on the earth and in the air.

" 'Lucifer, with a very great number of demons will be unchained from hell. By degrees they shall abolish the faith, even among persons consecrated to God. They shall blind them in such a manner that, without very special graces, these persons shall imbibe the spirit of those wicked angels. Many religious houses will entirely lose the faith, and shall be the cause of the loss of many persons. In the monasteries, the Flowers of the Church, will mould and rot. The superiors of religious communities should be alert regarding the ones they take into the community, for the devil will use all malice, to bring persons into the orders who are addicted to sin.

" 'Bad people will abound upon the earth; and the spirit of darkness shall spread over the earth a universal relaxation about everything relating to the service of God. Satan shall have very great power over nature (God's punishment for the crimes of men); temples will be erected for the worship of these demons. Some persons shall be transported from one place to another by these wicked spirits, even some priests, because these will not be animated by the Holy Spirit of the gospel, which is a spirit of humility, charity, and zeal for the glory of God.

" 'Some will make the dead rise and appear as holy persons. The souls of the damned shall also be summoned, and shall appear as united to their bodies. (Such persons, resurrected through the agency of demons, shall assume the figure of holy persons, who are known to have been upon earth, in order more easily to deceive them. These self-styled resuscitated persons shall be nothing but demons under their forms. In this way they shall preach a Gospel contrary to that of Jesus Christ, denying the existence of heaven.)

" 'In every place there shall be seen extraordinary prodigies, because the true faith has been extinguished, and a pale light shines in the world.

" 'My Son's Vicar shall have much to suffer, because for a time the Church shall be exposed to very great persecutions. This shall be the time of darkness. The Church shall have to pass through an awful crisis. France, Italy, Spain, and England shall have civil war. Blood shall flow through the streets. French shall fight French. Italians against Italians. After this there will be a frightful general war. For a time God shall not remember France, nor Italy (for two years or for one?), because the gospel of Jesus Christ is no more understood. The Holy Father will suffer much. I will be with Him to the end to receive His sacrifice. The wicked shall many times attempt His life.

" 'Nature demands vengeance against men, and she trembles with fright in expectation of what will befall the earth sullied with crimes. Tremble, O earth! And tremble you also who make profession of serving Jesus Christ, but inwardly worship yourselves, because God has delivered you to his enemies, because corruption is in holy places.

" 'In the year 1865[1] the abomination shall be seen in holy places, in convents, and then the demon shall make himself as the king of hearts. It will be about that time that Antichrist shall be born (1865). At his birth he shall vomit blasphemies. He shall have teeth; in a word, he shall be like an incarnate demon; he shall utter frightful screams; he shall work prodigies; and he shall feed on impure things. He shall have brothers, who, though not incarnate demons like him, shall nevertheless be children of iniquity. At the age of twelve years they shall have become remarkable for valiant victories, which they shall achieve; very soon each of them will be at the head of armies. Paris shall be burned, and Marseilles shall be submerged; many great cities shall be shattered and swallowed up by earthquakes. The populace will believe that everything is lost, will see nothing but murder, and will hear only the clang of arms and sacrilegious blasphemies.

" 'I address a pressing appeal to the earth. I call upon the true disciples of the living God, who reigns in the heavens; I call upon the true imitators of Christ made man, the only true Saviour of mankind; I call upon my children, those who are truly devoted to me, those who have offered themselves to me that I may lead them to My Son, those whom I carry as it were in my arms, those who have been animated by My spirit. Finally, I call on the apostles of these last days, these faithful disciples of Jesus Christ, who have lived despising the world and themselves, in poverty and humility, in contempt and in silence, in prayer and mortification, in chastity and union with God, in suffering and unknown to the world. It is time for them to come out and enlighten the world. Go ye forth and manifest yourselves as my darling children; I am with you and within you, so that your faith may be the light which illumines you in these unhappy days, and that your zeal may make you long for the glory and honor of the Most High. Fight, ye children of

---

[1] Whenever dates occur in prophecies they must be taken as conditional. By carrying out the requests of heaven any threatened event can be delayed, lessened, or completely canceled.

light; combat, ye small band that can see, for this is the time of times, the end of ends.

" 'The seasons of the year will change, the earth will produce only bad fruits, the stars will depart from their regular course, the moon will give only a weak, reddish light. Water and fire in the interior of the earth will rage violently and cause terrible earthquakes, whereby mountains and cities will sink into the depths. Earthquakes will also devour whole countries. Together with the Antichrist the demons will work great false miracles on earth and in the air. Voices will be heard in the air. Then men will desert religion and become worse and worse. Men will let themselves be deceived because they refused to adore the real Christ Who lives bodily amongst them. Woe to the inhabitants of the earth! Bloody wars, famines, pestilence and contagious diseases will develop. Terrible rain and hail will come with animals falling from the heavens, thunder and lightning burning down entire cities. The whole universe will be gripped by fear. Finally the sun will be darkened and faith alone will give light.

" 'A certain precursor of Antichrist, together with his followers from many nations, will fight the real Christ, the only Saviour of the world. He will endeavor to eliminate the adoration of God in order to be considered as God himself. Much blood will flow. Then the earth will be visited by all kinds of blows, from constant wars until the last war which finally will be made by the ten kings of the Antichrist.

" 'During the time of the arrival of Antichrist, the gospel will be preached everywhere, and all peoples and nations will then recognize the Truth.

" 'Rome will lose the faith and become the seat of Antichrist. Yet the Heathen Rome will disappear. See, here is the Beast with its subjects that claims to be the Saviour of the world. Proudly it rises in the air to go straight to Heaven, but it will be strangled by the Archangel Michael and cast down. And the earth, which for the past three days was in continuous convulsions, opens her fiery jaws and swallows him with all his cohorts forever into its hellish abyss. Eventually will water and fire cleanse the earth and the works of human pride will be destroyed and all will be renewed. Then will all serve God and glorify Him.

" 'The just will have much to suffer; their prayers, works of penance and tears will ascend to heaven. All of God's people will cry for forgiveness and grace and beg my help and intercession. Then Jesus Christ will command His angels, by a special act of His Justice and Mercy, to deliver all His enemies to death. Then suddenly all persecutors of the Church of Jesus Christ and all evil doers will perish, and rest and peace between God and man will appear. Jesus Christ will be served, adored and glorified. Love of neighbor will begin to flourish all over. The new kings will be on the right hand of the Church which will grow strong, and which will be humble, pious, poor, zealous and followers of the virtues. All over, the Gospel will now be preached, people will make great progress in faith; there will be unity amongst the laborers of Jesus Christ, and people will live in the fear of God.

" 'Behold the reign of the ten kings! Woe to the inhabitants of the earth; there shall be sanguinary wars, and famine, and plagues, and contagious maladies; there shall be showers of a frightful hail of animals; thunder shall shake entire cities; earthquakes which shall swallow up some countries; voices shall be heard in the air; men (in despair) shall knock their heads against the walls; they shall call on death; and death shall be their torment; blood shall flow from every side. Who shall be able to overcome (all these evils)? Fire shall rain from heaven, and shall destroy three cities. The whole world shall be struck with terror, and many will allow themselves to be seduced, because they have not believed the true Christ living among them. The sun becomes dark. Faith only shall survive. So the time! The abyss opens. Behold the king of kings of darkness! Behold the beast with his subjects! . . .' "

Chapter 15

Triumphant Peace

The most profound statement that has been given to mankind since Christ's Ascension into Heaven is the promise of His Blessed Mother at Fatima: "IN THE END, MY IMMACULATE HEART WILL TRIUMPH AND A PERIOD OF PEACE WILL BE GRANTED TO HUMANITY." This statement gives the key to what man can expect from the year 1917 to the time of the first judgment.

Most people believe that her promised peace is merely a cessation of war, but it is much more than that. It will be a peace such as the world has never known. It will be peace for all humanity. It will be ABSOLUTE PEACE.

To most Americans, peace means military peace followed by an uninterrupted flow of profitable materialism. We have seen two world wars come to an end and military peace follow and have seen prosperity skyrocket; but we also witnessed world evil as never before. Our Blessed Mother's peace means not only the end of war, which is punishment for evil, but also the complete and final end of evil. It means nothing less than the TRIUMPHANT REIGN OF HER SON.

When Our Lady said: "My Immaculate Heart will triumph" she could only mean triumph over evil. Mary's peace, when it comes will be a period in time without evil. If Mary Immaculate wished to be more specific, I believe this is what she could have told us: "The 'End' I refer to is the end of the sixth day of creation when God will stop co-creating men, when He will orderly end the SO-CALLED POPULATION EXPLOSION. He will then bring on the next era which will be a period of complete rest and peace. Before doing this, the world must be completely rid of wickedness and evil. The end of evil is to be 'My triumph'. Thereafter, all lovers of My Son who remain faithful during the passion and crucifixion of His Mystical Body under the Antichrist, will live as men and women, companions for each other, enjoying the quality of peace and happiness which God intended for the Garden of Eden."

* * *

In the beginning, God created heaven and earth at which time myriads of angels gave Him glory in heaven in love with souls and knowledge. On the sixth day of creation, we read in Genesis, He created man like unto His Son. God breathed upon His new creation and a speck of His divinity entered the body, thus giving it soul and knowledge like unto the angels, but also a body with five senses. This new being lost knowledge, however, when he sinned and has striven ever since to recover it with his intellect. This creature could glorify Him in two ways like the angels but also in a new way with external senses by seeing, hearing, smelling, tasting and touching.

God placed man on earth in the midst of a paradise where He intended man would glorify his Creator forever. In this state of joy he had no other desire than to praise, love and obey Him. God took delight in His newly created being. He gave him freely all the fruits found in this earthly paradise. There would be no death to put an end to his happiness.

This man possessed a body which was free from the limitations placed on him after his fall. It was free from the incarceration of the animal flesh. This spiritualized body had power of agility which is penetration. It had power of impassibility which is freedom from pain and sickness. It had power of immortality which is freedom from death. God put only one restriction upon him — man must prove worthy of His great love and goodness. He could partake of everything in paradise except the fruit of the tree of knowledge of good and evil; of that tree he must not eat.

God saw that man needed a companion and helpmate and created woman to provide this. THEY WOULD BE TWO IN ONE FLESH, both glorifying Him in all they did. The delight of His love permeating their bodies was a reward for faithfulness in serving Him in a three-fold way.

God, seeing that His plan of man and woman was good, decreed that through them there would be more human beings to glorify Him. He instructed these new creatures to cooperate in bringing forth other human beings. He actually gave them the great privilege of joining with God in co-creation. This would be a second purpose for their existence. In bringing forth children, God-man-woman would join AS A TRINITY to carry out His purpose of having ever more beings to glorify Him. God-man-woman have since been co-creating the human race. For this reason it could be that the sixth day of creation has not yet ended. When God, as co-Creator, will have sufficient human beings to glorify Him, it would seem He will dispense with the secondary purpose — putting an end to co-creation without, in any way affecting man's primary purpose of loving, serving, and obeying Him in the three-fold way.

Lucifer, the proud angel who was cast from heaven for the sin of self-love, became infuriated with this new plan of Almighty God for a being that could love and glorify Him in a three-fold way, while angels without bodies were able to glorify God in only two ways. Deprived of what his intellect knew to be a highly desirable existence, he determined to prevent it. Intent upon upsetting this plan for the glory of God, he approached the innocent child-like woman and deceived her by denying that she would die the death if she ate of the tree of knowledge. She did eat the forbidden fruit and gave it to her companion who ate also, thus committing the original sin.

Lucifer's greatest success came when he employed the power of confusion. Using this instrument, he could bring great numbers under his spell at one stroke, such as in the sixteenth century when he organized confusion inside Christ's church. Ever since he has employed confusion until today one-half the people of the world are living under a godless plan of existence with the other half of the world's population almost as godless while still living under the protection of governments founded on Christian principles.

At no time has Lucifer been so successful as in the twentieth century. It is obvious to all students of our time that the devil has succeeded in leading most Christian countries to decay. All signs of the times confirm the warnings of Our Lord and His Mother that we are living in the last days — that the days of the Apocalypse are passing by — and that man is traveling the road that leads to death.

We are told that the world will not immediately end after the Antichrist. We are told the "earth will be remade." We have not been told in what state man will live on earth after His coming. Men and women are deeply concerned with what the future will bring, especially those of us who believe we are to take part in ringing out the old age of sin, pain, and sorrow, and bringing in Mary's Triumphant Peace.

The author, at this point in his book, gives his own opinion of what is to come. It is entirely a personal opinion arrived at through reasoning after reading the signs of the times and interpreting them in the light of the wisdom in the Bible. After years of studying this subject, I am convinced and solemnly believe the following will occur in the lives of many living today:

1. I believe that the momentous events of the final drama of Christianity are now upon us, with each morning newspaper describing the passing show. That the 'last days' spoken of by St. Louis de Montfort shortly after the year 1700, started off in 1830 when Our Blessed Lady appeared to Sister Catherine Laboure, and have been in progress ever since; that the last of the 'last days' commenced in 1914 when Kaiser Wilhelm went to war. Just what day, month or year, the unfulfilled apocalyptic events will occur is not known — God knows — but that they will occur in the fulness of His plan and during the remaining years of the twentieth century is my solemn belief. Time for God is entirely relative. At best, dates given by Him to mystics are approximate dates, indicating a period of time and not an exact day or year. However, the pattern of time seems to have been established fifty years ago when He permitted World War One to break out on August 2, 1914. I believe the final crucifixion of the Mystical Body of Christ will follow the pattern of the crucifixion of His human body on Calvary. For each day He suffered His private passion, the crucifixion of the Whole Body may be for one year's time instead of one day's time, as on Calvary. The 1260 days of the reign of Antichrist can

THE LAST WORLD WAR

definitely be the 3½ years of public passion of Christ's whole church on earth. Christ's private passion started when He went into the desert to fast and pray for 40 days to prepare for His coming crucifixion. I believe a comparable passion of the Mystical Body is upon us now in the form of world wars, depressions and general confusion; that Christ will surrender His Mystical Body for trial, judgment and the second crucifixion; that Antichrist will be released to direct this diabolical persecution of Christ's Church, which will last three and one-half years. It will end when the beast is chained in hell. The Resurrection of the Mystical Body will follow. Then Christ will come in glory.

2. I believe at the time Antichrist is given his brief acknowledgement, his short reign as prince of the World, that our fight against him will be primarily of the spirit; that he will attempt to take his place in the hearts of all men in a supreme effort to take us away from God. Our suffering will be, for the most part, the torment of the soul. There will be no hiding from him or his diabolical assistants. They will be everywhere. He will use man's LOVE OF THE WORLD AND THE THINGS IN IT to achieve his end. This spiritual battle in America will be staged around WEALTH, MATERIAL POSSESSIONS AND INTELLECTUAL PRIDE — already so prevalent.

3. I believe that as the last days come to an end so will the sixth day of creation. To bring this about His whole Mystical Body must carry the cross. We, His members, who remain faithful and who may die at the hands of the Antichrist will go as martyrs to heaven to return in relatively short time to recover our bodies, and in a spiritualized state to meet Our Lord in glory on earth. Those who do not die WILL BE CLAD IN IMMORTALITY WITHOUT EVER DYING.

4. I believe that between this persecution and the coming of Christ Our Blessed Mother's triumphant peace will come;

that it is to be the time of the One Fold and the One Shepherd, and that mankind is rapidly approaching this stupendous reality; that, as Christ after His Resurrection stayed forty days on earth, His Mystical Body will remain on earth for the period of Mary's triumphant peace and then be taken as a unit into heaven at the General Resurrection and the Last Judgment.

5. I believe that during Mary's time of peace, men and women will live in a paradise on earth in uninterrupted peace and happiness as was intended by God in the beginning; that the Elect will live within the church triumphant in the same state as was to be enjoyed originally by Adam and Eve.

6. I believe because of His mercy, those who, through ignorance and false doctrine, love Him imperfectly, will be detained in purgatory during the triumphant peace; but that the enemies of Our Lord, members of Satan's diabolical mystical body will drop into hell during the three days of darkness when the Battle of Armageddon is fought.

All this — I do believe; and believe it so confidently, as a human conviction, that I dare to publish it for others to share with me.

THE UNION OF CHRIST AND HIS MOTHER

Our Blessed Mother is reported by the Marianhill Fathers, Detroit, to have appeared in 1943 in the town of Girkalnis, a part of the war zone between Russia and East Prussia. She is said to have appeared three times, Feb. 8, Feb. 15, and on March 17. She settled in a cloud above the tabernacle in the village church. All present in the church saw Her, and testimony that followed is in agreement. In Her arms was Her Divine Son. In the cloud were brilliant stars. The stars were believed to be symbols for saints. She spoke little but did say: "I am the Mother of Mercy, and I wish to be known by that name." She answered the question, "How long will you remain with us?": "I will remain with you to the end." This appearance of Our Blessed Mother is believed to have been for the purpose of making known that she reigns with her Son on earth, as she reigns beside Him in Heaven on the throne of God. Catholic literature, highly regarded, confirms this union of the Mystical Body of Christ in the Sacrament of the Eucharist.

In the well known book, *This Tremendous Lover*, by M. Eugene Boylan, O. Cist. R. can be found on page 151:

"The immediate effect of this Sacrament (of the Holy Eucharist) is to unite us to Christ, but it also unites us to all His members, for we are all one body. It unites us to the Blessed Virgin, to all the Saints, to all the Souls in Purgatory, to all living members of the Church."

In the Encyclical — The Mystical Body of Christ by Pope Pius XII June 29, 1943 — "The close union of the Mystical Body of Jesus Christ with its Head . . . reaches, as it were, a climax in the Holy Eucharist . . . "

Mary Agreda gives us these consoling words:

Jesus Christ while speaking before those who witnessed His ascension into Heaven said to them: "My sweetest children, I am about to ascend to my Father, from whose bosom I descended in order to rescue and save men. I leave with you in my stead my own Mother as your Protectress, Consoler and Advocate. All of you shall have her as your Mother, as your Superior and Head, and so shall also your successors. She shall answer your doubts and solve your difficulties; in her, those who seek Me shall always find Me; for I SHALL REMAIN IN HER UNTIL THE END OF THE WORLD, and I AM IN HER NOW, although you do not understand how." — *The City of God*, by Sister Mary of Agreda — year 1617 — Page 765, in the volume on the Transfixion.

REPORTS OF RECENT APPARITIONS
Seredne (Ukraine) and Garabandal (Spain)

A Ukrainian monthly magazine, *The Light*, published by the Basilian Fathers in Toronto, Canada, brought to Americans an account of a series of apparitions that reportedly took place in Seredne from December 20, 1954, through November 21, 1955. There were twenty apparitions in all. Because of the harassment of the Communist Government, the ecclesiastical authorities have been hampered in their efforts to investigate

The four Garabandel children shortly after the start of the Appartitions in the summer of 1961. From left to right: Maria Dolores, Conchita, Maria-Cruz, Jacinta.

these reports thoroughly. However, in content like the apparitions of Fatima, the warnings are urgent. They speak of great danger to Rome and the Holy Father (though the principals in the apparitions interpret this to mean a spiritual crisis rather than a physical danger) and plead again with the people to amend their lives and devote themselves to penance.

More recent still, and as yet incomplete, are the apparitions and the locutions granted to four children of San Sebastian de Garabandal, a village in Spain. The four children — all girls — were eleven and twelve years of age when these visitations began, June 18, 1961. St. Michael appeared to the girls and prepared them for the later appearances of Our Lady, the first of which took place on June 25 of that same month. Since that time hundreds of apparitions have been granted to the children, who are always seen to go into a rapture at the time of the visions. Some witnesses have numbered as many as 2300 such visitations. There have been as many as seven in one day. The message is again that of La Salette and Fatima, with special emphasis on devotion to the Holy Eucharist.

"There must be many sacrifices, much penance. There must be many visits to the Blessed Sacrament. But first of all, we must be very good. If we are not, a punishment will fall on us. Already the cup is filling. If we do not change, the punishment will be very great."

This message was given on July 14, 1961, but the recipient was instructed to keep it secret until October 17, when she revealed it to her pastor.

The ecclesiastical authorities have kept close watch on these apparitions and though no definite stand for or against them has been taken as yet, it is known that the Holy Office on July 28, 1965, instructed the local Bishop "to follow with a vigilant eye all future developments . . . and to kindly report (all future developments) to the Holy Office."

The children have been instructed that two great events will occur in the world to alert mankind; the first will have worldwide repercussions, the second will be local at Garabandal. However, this second will be greater than the prodigy of the sun at Fatima (Portugal) in 1917. The date for this second event is known to the children, who have confided it also to their Bishop. They will announce the date eight days before the event. If this latter miracle does not bring about a conversion in the world, then a third and very destructive heaven-sent blow will fall on mankind. Much that has been revealed in Spain cannot yet be published, but in time, if the examinations now under way verify the heavenly nature of these events, the world will know about them.[1]

THE LAST WARNING

Direct from Heaven

St. Michael the Archangel appeared to Conchita on the night of Friday, June 18, as she had prophesied, after Our Lady had appeared to her on December 8, 1964, and again on January 1,

---

[1] This information is taken from a small brochure "The Apparitions at Garabandal" published by the Carmelite Press, Whitefriars, Faversham, Kent, with the Imprimatur of the Vicar General of the diocese, December 22, 1964.

1965, and gave her the following message from Our Lady.

"As my Message of October 18, 1961, has not been complied with and as little has been done to make it known, I am telling you that this is the last one. Previously the cup was filling up; now it is brimming over. Many priests are following the road to eternal perdition and taking many souls with them. Ever less importance is being given to the Eucharist. We should turn away the anger of God by our own efforts. If you ask His pardon, with a sincere heart, He will grant it. I, Your Mother, through the medium of the Archangel St. Michael, wish to tell you that you should make amends. You have now received the last warning. I love you very much and I do not wish you to be damned. Ask sincerely for forgiveness and We will give it to you. You should make more sacrifices and think more about the Passion of Jesus. June 18, 1965."

(Signed) Conchita Gonzalez

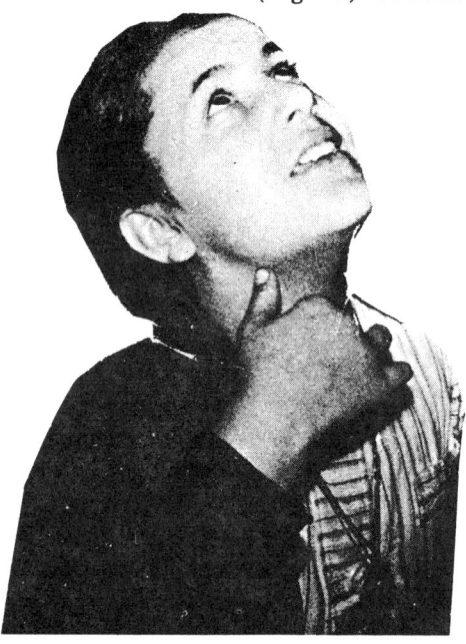

Maria Dolores making the sign of the cross at the end of a rapture while saying goodbye to Our lady, whom she sees above.

THE END OF THE MODERN WORLD

One of the penetrating minds of our age, Romano Guardini,[1] has described his views of the coming generation, in chapters on the dissolution of the modern world and the preview of the world to come. He is making "an attempt to orient oneself within the tangled or fluid situation which still marks our age." He develops the ideas more at length in *Briefer vom Comer See* (1927), *Welt und Person*, (1937), and *Freiheit, Gnade, Schiksal* (1948).

"Faith," he writes, "will maintain itself against animosity and danger. At the forefront of Christian life, man's obedience to God will assert itself with a new power. Knowing that the very last thing is at stake, that he has reached that extremity which only obedience could meet . . . man will practice a pure obedience. Christianity will arm itself for an illiberal stand directed unconditionally toward Him Who is unconditioned. Its illiberalism will differ from every form of violence, however, because it will be an act of freedom, an unconditional obedience to God. . .

"If I am right in my conclusions about the coming world, the Old Testament will take on a new significance. The Old Testament reveals the Living God Who smashes the mythical bonds of the earth, Who casts down the powers and the pagan rulers of life; it shows us the man of faith who is obedient to the acts of God according to the terms of the Covenant. These Old Testament truths will grow in meaning and import. The stronger the demonic powers the more crucial will be that 'victory over the world' realized in freedom and through Faith . . .

"If we understand the eschatalogical text of Holy Writ correctly, trust and courage will totally form the character of the last age. The surrounding 'Christian' culture and the traditions supported by it will lose their effectiveness. That loss will belong to the danger given by scandal, that danger of which it is said: it will, if possible, deceive even the elect.' (Matt. 24:24)

"Loneliness in faith will be terrible. Love will disappear from the face of the public world (Matt. 23:12), but the more precious will that love be which flows from one lonely person to another,

---

[1] Guardini, Romano, *The End of the Modern World,* Sheed and Ward, New York, 1956, 131-132

involving a courage of the heart born from the immediacy of the love of God as it was made known in Christ... Perhaps love will achieve an intimacy and harmony never known to this day..."

THE CULLIGAN FAMILY

"Suffer little children to come unto me, and forbid them not."

Chapter 16

A Message to Our Children

THE LAST WILL AND TESTAMENT OF EMMETT AND ANNA CULLIGAN

Dear Children:

We have seen many wonderful things. We have known and lived with the finest people. It is true we have lived in a world filled with sin, but we have also lived next door to saints.

Our married life, under God's providence, in which we placed our complete Faith, has been one of dramatic adventure. We never recognized so-called trouble. We looked upon it as a challenge which made life more interesting. Your mother once said: "We are bigger than trouble." Each of you were welcomed with serene anticipation. The seven trips to maternity hospitals in Model T Fords were journeys of true joy. When John was coming we ran out of gas; with Gerald we were caught in a heavy fog.

Not one of our children ever caused either their mother or their father a heartache. As we look back, we can remember a great many arguments among our children, but never a lasting disagreement or misunderstanding. Our home was one in which love reigned. God has been very good to all of us, as He is to all families who place their complete trust in His providence. What a great God-given privilege it is for a mother and a father to be co-creators with God Himself. Our marital union of 46 years has increased the communion of saints with 42 souls. There is no other achievement in all history that equals parenthood, especially when all one's progeny remain forever within Christ's Mystical Body.

Your forefathers, for a thousand years or more, were tillers of the soil. They grew their own food, obtained milk directly from the cow, churned their butter by hand, made their cloth and clothes. As children, we witnessed these homely tasks. On a summer Sunday, after Mass, the whole congregation of neighbors would retire unannounced to the Linnans, O'Learys, Fitzpatricks, Culligans, Kings, Courtneys, Deegons, Ryles or to any one of the many farm homes of simple country folks who came West to "break sod." John Linnan, who visited in our home recently, still farms his land which he "took up" with your great-grandfather Culligan near Maurice, Iowa, in 1873. He was hale and hearty in 1956. Your grandmother's folks — the Sullivans — have continuously lived on and farmed their Iowa land near the Trappist Monastery at Garryowen since 1846.

These pioneer people, on their free Sundays, entertained themselves with natural amusements. One could hear waves of laughter a half mile away, coming from a shady lawn on a summer afternoon. The "women folks," all working together, would stir up a Sunday dinner for as many as 50 in no time; the like of which, for quality and quantity, could not be found today. The children played (your mother and father were neighbor children) unaided by gadgets other than a baseball and a bat, or a pony. Toward evening, young and old would sing, dance or recite tall tales. Everyone believed in God — and He showered His blessings upon the whole countryside.

Your own father desired to follow his father's way of life, and at the age of ten was making plans to spend his life on the land. He considered farming a noble Christian profession; noble because it required honest physical labor. Of all the occupations by which a father can make a living for a large family, none is better than agriculture; none gives more peaceful satisfaction; none is more becoming to the dignity of a free man; or none more constructive for the proper development of a family. "Oh, happy husbandmen, did they but know their blessings." God intended that the land be home for His children. Your father had a farm ready for his bride. Our two oldest children were born there. However the devastating results of World War I took our lands, and also the legacy that your grandparents assembled through frugal pioneering in America. We were forced to leave our home, in the country, to take up urban living in a busy world ill of the disease of atheistic materialism.

We did the best we could under the stern rules to provide a home, a living, and education for our children. We had explicit faith in God's providence. Our prayer always was: "Give us today our daily bread" — and He always did.

We have all been many places. We have had the opportunity to use the marvelous devices resulting from man's ingenuity. We have been as happy as any family could be on earth. And, now, it is our destiny to live through the Age of the Apocalypse into the age of the One Fold and One Shepherd.

It now becomes plain that Christ, in His parable of the wheat and cockle, planned a growing season of something over nineteen centuries during which time man was given free will, which developed such moral decay that the world could not much longer go on under man's planning. God permitted greed, injustice, world-wide apostasy, atheistic materialism, and just plain sin to abound, in the same world, in which his friends lived. It required great vigilance on the part of the good not to be smothered by the cockle. And, now, at the time of Apocalypse, both cockle and grain are to be cut, with the weeds to be separated and cast into the fire. The harvest is surely overripe in 1966, and the sickles will soon cut away. Christ, during the remaining days of our era, will offer His Mystical Body to be persecuted by Antichrist, so all of us can atone to His Father for our own sins and for the sins of the world.

OUR DEAR CHILDREN: WE BEQUEATH TO YOU OUR OWN FAITH and the Faith of our fathers—which reaches back through 15 centuries to the days of St. Patrick. Your people all through the ages, have always kept the faith; the Harringtons, the O'Learys, the Kelleys, the Murrays, the Guinans, the Culligans, the Courtneys, and the Sullivans. Your forefathers, and their neighbors in Ireland, kept Christianity constantly alive in all the corners of the earth. For 1500 years they have sent untold thousands of their sons and daughters as religious to foreign lands. In 1966 there still go from Ireland, every month, many religious to carry on the work of God, never again to return to their homes except for rare visits. We give you also the Faith we, ourselves, have in God, the Father Almighty. We give you a Faith which believes all the revelations that have predicted the days in which we live.

The Culligans visit Pope Paul

GO RIGHT ON WITH YOUR WAY OF LIFE; continue your routine tasks; judge no one; diligently prepare your souls for the great adventure ahead. Take joy in the anticipation of being present to greet Him as He descends from Heaven. The best preparation for lay people is the recitation of the Rosary. Recite it once daily, as a family group and often, alone, during the day. Hear Mass and receive Communion every day you can. When there is no public Mass, endeavor to hear it underground. Be very sure to be constantly in the state of grace.

IT IS OUR GREAT DESIRE that all of us stand up one at a time, whenever the Christian roll is called, and shout: "Here," and exclaim with joy, "I am a Son of God!" It may cost our lives to do this, but this is our destiny, and also our glorious privilege. WE DESIRE THAT OUR WHOLE FAMILY BECOME SAINTS. When we meet Christ together, your father and mother look forward to His greeting us thus: "Oh yes, of course . . . I often heard Mother speak of the Culligan family."

WE HAVE ALREADY GIVEN YOU the most precious of all gifts that a mother and father can give their children — that of Life itself. And, now, as we approach the end of our lives, we can see plainly how we will live throughout eternity. By giving you Life, we gave you the glorious adventure of Life Eternal, the mysteries of which we will all soon understand.

As to the little mundane treasures that we have lovingly accumulated in our home during our 46 years of married life, we consider these of so little importance now, that they hardly are worthy of mention here.

So, our dear children, Mary and James, Catherine and Eugene, Jeanne and Thomas, Anna-Marie and Burt, Marjorie and Jude, Joyce and John, and Father Kevin, and our 35 grandchildren — all of us take heart to be courageously strong for the days ahead: THINK BIG, LOVE MUCH, TALK LITTLE, GIVE FREELY, DO NOT WORRY, SAY THE ROSARY, AND BE KIND.

And, may God have mercy on the souls of all our people, living and dead!

OUR DAUGHTER MARY DIED ON THE EVE OF THE QUEENSHIP OF MARY

On May 30, 1966, at ten minutes to six on the eve of the Feast of the Queenship of the Mother of God, at the time to start vespers in Heaven, Our Lady called at the home of the Caterina family at San Diego to take their wife and mother to be present at the greatest feast day in Heaven. Mary had been silently bearing the agonies of cancer over a three year period, offering her suffering for the sins in our evil world. She had been anointed four times, once by her brother, Very Reverend Kevin Culligan, O.C.D. Suddenly, her life in this world ended and she was taken off for the greatest of all adventures — that of passing from one world to an entirely different world — a never ending world of joy, to be among all the saints. We now have one of our seven children a saint in Heaven, close by Our Lady whom Mary loved so much. At Mary's rosary at St. Martin's Church the evening before her funeral, there were assembled over one thousand friends and neighbors from throughout California and beyond. The next morning five hundred people attended the funeral mass. It was a day of joy for her mother and father. Thanks be to God!

Epilogue

Anna and Emmett Culligan, Father Hannon, Joyce and John Culligan on porch of ranch home at Yellowstone.

Chapter 17

Our Eight Years in the Mountains

I took my family to the mountains in 1951 following the advice of the Apostle, Matthew, Ch. 24:16, in which he advised at the time of the "abomination of desolation" that we drop everything and head for the hills. I took this advice seriously. I had been reading the manuscript of the Jesuit Father, Reverend F. J. Bunse, S. J., in which he reviewed the exorcisms by Father Theophilus Riesinger O.F.M., Cap., at Earling, Iowa in 1928. Earling is a small town near the community where many of my people and the folks of Mrs. Culligan lived for almost a century. At the time of these exorcisms, the whole countryside was excited with what was taking place in the Earling church and convent of the parish buildings on top of the Earling hill. I believed the prophecies resulting from these exorcisms by Father Theophilus would occur as foretold. As the father of a large family, I considered it my duty to go into hiding in the mountains to prepare for the coming of the Antichrist.

I searched for land in Montana; and at 6500 feet, on the borders of Yellowstone Park, found land which suited my purpose. I bought the ranch and immediately started building. I put up sufficient living quarters to care for thirty people. I also included a house for religious, with a family chapel fully equipped for daily Mass and perpetual adoration. As soon as the buildings were ready, in the early spring each year the Culligans would assemble at our retreat and live there in peace and tranquility. We had my dear friend, Father Joseph Hannon, O.S.B., assigned to serve our mountain retreat by the Right Reverend Ignatius Hunkler, O.S.B., Abbot of Assumption Abbey, Richardton, North Dakota. Father Hannon had been a professor of mine at the College of St. Thomas in St. Paul, Minnesota, when I was a

Father Albert Joseph Hannon, O.S.B.

boy. He was a saintly, humble American pioneer priest with a remarkable memory. He loved the mountains. During his long life, he spent much time as an Indian missionary in various locations in the Rocky Mountains. He was delighted with his assignment as chaplain for the Culligan family. We had many priests and bishops visit the ranch during the years we were there. Many mornings we would have four and five Masses following one another. For 30 days, we had as our guest the great French musician from Paris, Dr. Francois Lefevre, a Doctor of Gregorian Chant. One morning we had four bishops as guests and the doctor undertook, as a one man choir, to give each bishop a special Gregorian mass — and did so. The last bishop afterward said to him: "Doctor Lefevre, I didn't think it was possible for you to bring up a fourth Gregorian Mass for me." These were happy days for all of the Culligans.

Our youngest son, Gerald, spent his summers with us as he progressively went through the Jesuit Seattle University. During his last summer, he told his parents that he was going to be a priest. Early in June, 1955, he bade the family goodbye and boarded the North Coast Limited for Boston, where he entered the Discalced Carmelite Seminary. From that day, for eight years, to the day of his ordination, he never left the seminary for a visit home. He was ordained in the summer of 1963.

When he was to receive first orders on August 15, 1959, the whole family left the ranch to go to Holy Hill, Wisconsin to attend the ceremonies. Two days later, on August 17, 1959, as we were returning homeward, the Montana Earthquake struck at 11:37 at night. None of the family was at home, although Father Hannon, our faithful maid, Lenora Reed, and three ranch employees, were fast asleep when "all hell broke loose." I would rather let Father Hannon describe that night — and he will pick up after me.

When we surveyed our loss, which was complete, I realized it was the work of Divine Providence. It so happened that the epicenter of the earthquake, which had a radius of 200 miles, was placed by government geologists in the Culligan front yard. As I saw the great ruins of our loving work, I decided that God Almighty and His Blessed Mother wanted us to come out of hiding, and be among those who must actively carry on during the dramatic days to come. So we used a bulldozer to gather all the debris into one great pile, and had a huge bonfire.

As Father Theophilus gave his opinion that Antichrist would come in 1955, and Father Bunse, S.J., followed along with him, I did also. But Antichrist didn't come on their schedule, and after five years had passed, I realized that prophecies cannot place correct dates on coming events. We went back to our city home in California to await the coming of the Antichrist, which I am sure will occur in the remaining days of the 20th Century.

I am now convinced that the birth of the Antichrist has been foretold, and that he is alive, and in the summer of 1966 is four years of age. I decided, therefore, to rewrite "The Last World War", revising the 9th edition to its present form. We now await the evil one's coming at home — this time without fear. Father Joseph, take over:

Father Kevin's First Mass — June 22, 1963

THE MONTANA EARTHQUAKE
An eye witness description of the disaster
By Father Joseph Albert Hannon O.S.B.
Catholic Chaplain of Blarneystone Ranch (age 84)

There have been many accounts of the disastrous earthquake that convulsed the extreme southwestern section of Montana on August 17 and 18, 1959. Nearly all of these descriptions deal with the awful tragedy of Hegben Dam, the scene of the loss of many lives. Naturally, a story about that locality attracts more attention than would a place where no lives were lost. A very severe earthquake struck Blarneystone, as can be attested by those living in that section. When the temblor struck, I was in bed in one of the houses.

The town of West Yellowstone is located at the western entrance of Yellowstone Park. About ten miles to the north and one mile off the highway leading to Ennis and past Lake Hegben, stands a cluster of buildings, one of which is locally known as "Blarney Castle" located on a cattle ranch named "Blarneystone Ranch." As one approaches the first building, one comes to a large imposing structure consisting of a commodious living room, a dining room, a kitchen and the cook's quarters on the first floor. On the second floor are two large bedrooms and a bath. A few feet away stands another building of equal dimensions. On the first floor are two large bedrooms and a bath. On the second, the chapel and the chaplain's quarters. Some fifty yards farther on is a smaller structure and this was occupied by a young couple and their small children. The man is an employee of the ranch. All the structures are solidly built and sumptuously furnished. Lower down toward Grayling Creek, which runs through the ranch, are other buildings for the cattle on the ranch. This ranch is the property of Emmett and Anna Culligan of San Bernardino, California. Mr. Culligan and family spend the summer on the ranch and he, himself, visits it frequently at other times of the year. This property was acquired by Mr. Culligan nine years ago and he has spent much money, time and talent in building it up to where it has become one of the attractions of that section of Montana. I occupied the chaplain's quarters on the eventful night of August 17. I was alone in the house. Mr. and Mrs. Culligan were in Milwaukee attending their youngest son's final induction into the Carmelite Order.

I retired about ten. I think I dropped off to sleep almost immediately. I have the impression that I awakened and looked at the clock. It was just 11:30. Almost at once, and without a moment's warning, came a dreadful roaring sound and the house seemed to be raised abruptly and dropped amid a fearful shaking. It was no swaying motion; it resembled a violent shaking. My bed began to spin around and heave violently. I thought the roof was about to fall. I swung around on my face and clung to the sides. I must have resembled a rodeo rider trying to stick on a bucking bronco. As all earthly things must come to an end, be they life or quake, the shaking finally ceased and I climbed out of bed. The electricity was off and there could be no light. I groped my way to the chapel and tried to open the door. It was blocked by some object against it. I finally succeeded in opening it. The chapel was a mess. The altar had up-ended and was in the middle of the room. I got hold of a candle and a match and made a light. Then, I went back to my room and dressed.

All this time the tremors continued at intervals of a few minutes but of less violence than the first. After I got dressed, I started to look for the others. I thought I heard Lenore, the colored cook, screaming. I found the two women and the little girls some distance from the buildings along the road. They had had the foresight to grab some blankets when they fled their beds and the buildings. It was most fortunate that they did so, for it was a chilly night. They took no time to don their clothes but rushed out as they were. The tremors continued at intervals every few minutes and at every fresh "shake," the colored mammy would cry out "O Lawd!"

A gentleman, a geologist from New York, who with his family was camping on the side of Grayling Creek opposite the buildings, came over to us accompanied by his men assistants. Being a 'geologist, he understood the activities of such phenomena. He advised us to stay out of the buildings, warning us that another and perhaps more severe shock might occur. This, he said, might demolish all the structures. We had a very interesting conference regarding the predicament we were in. However, I prevailed on him to permit me to go in and secure clothes for the women and children. He insisted on accompanying me. We went into the basement, where I found a lantern in good running order. He was already equipped with one, so we now had light. We ascended to the first floor and here he remained while I went up to the second floor where the chapel is located, the room that I was occupying. I procured what I considered necessary, including my breviary which is always most important.

We then went to the house already described as "the first." The big living room was a disastrous sight. All the pictures, statues, ornaments and bric-a-brac were strewn on the floor and broken to bits. The kitchen was a deplorable sight. Refrigerator and frigidaire were shaken from their places. Broken dishes, glassware, pots, pans and other objects littered the floor. The other rooms in both houses fared no better. We did not visit the cottage described as "the living quarters of Mr. and Mrs. Russel and their two small daughters." I understood that it was completely demolished and as it stands on the edge of the main fault and the embankment caused by a 16 foot fall of the earth at this point, there was a constant danger of it toppling over. I was much impressed by the behavior of young Mrs. Russel. All through the disaster she never uttered a complaint or manifested the least sign of fear or agitation. She is a jewel — a brave heart.

Now, for the subsequent activities, and to bring this hectic tale to a close. Let me make this one philosophical remark. That which took Mr. Culligan, at the expenditure of much energy, industry, talent and money, nine years to erect, was demolished in the space of nine seconds. The power of God and God's nature over the puny efforts of man was evident and everywhere.

Finally, John Russel (referred to above as an employee on the ranch) came with Mr. Culligan's car which was undamaged. We all climbed in. We started to go some place — where, no one had the slightest idea. As we drove toward the highway, we met Mrs. Morris who, with her husband, operates a string of tourist cabins. They also conduct a fine dining place. This lady kindly invited us to her headquarters. She said there was coffee being prepared. She also offered us the use of a very commodious cabin. She told us that the quake caused no damage in that cabin ex-

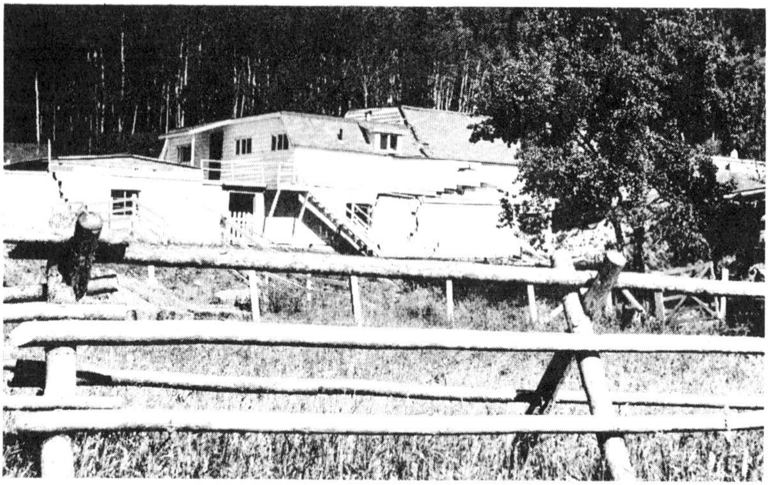

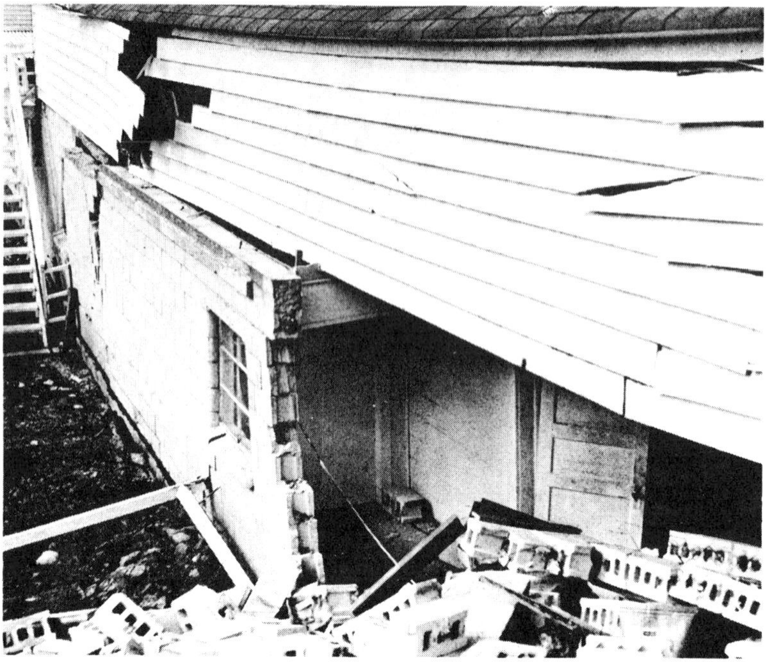

cept for a few utensils being shaken off their places. Their cabins are constructed of logs and very low, not so susceptible to shock. We thanked her and promised to return. When we reached the highway, we found others of the same mind as ourselves. They were in cars and were going where no one knew or seemed to care. Just to "get out." We soon found, however, that nobody was going "any place." The highway was obstructed by huge cracks, some five feet wide and of considerable depth. We saw one car up-ended with its nose in a fissure and the hind end pointing skyward. Highway patrolmen were on the job by this time and forbade all traffic.

We decided to take advantage of the good lady's invitation and drove to her place. Here we found a large crowd gathered who were drinking coffee prepared on an improvised fireplace outside the buildings. I was very graciously received by the crowd. They seemed glad to have a priest among them and I received several invitations to occupy a room in neighbors' cottages. However, I decided to stay with my crowd and we were given a very suitable cabin containing four rooms.

At dawn, we surveyed the tragedy of the night. The Blarneystone buildings that took nine years to build were a shamble beyond repair. When the first snow comes it is recommended that the ruins be burned and the ashes covered with a bulldozer. The geologists were excited to find at the great fault they had been exploring, tracing and mapping all summer, the south wall of the fault had fallen sixteen feet from the North or mountain side of the fault. The Culligan buildings were built astraddle the main fault and had dropped sixteen feet, too. The earth dropped all across the ranch land, at some points as much as twenty feet. This seems to be somewhat of a geological record. It can be said that the earth literally dropped beneath us.

At Grayling Creek, which is a mighty stream to be called a "creek," there was formed a new water fall. The fall is right smack at the concrete bridge which Cleo Marshall finished only three days before the quake. The bridge was the first of man's handiwork to drop over the falls. It lies as wreckage beneath this new cascade. No livestock was lost or injured. In fact, the quake seemed to increase egg production, for after the quake several more eggs were gathered than there were hens.

I wish here to pay tribute to Mr. and Mrs. Morris. They were extremely kind, attentive and considerate. I would like to get another opportunity to convey my personal appreciation and gratitude to them for their kindness. We returned to their dining room for breakfast. After this I retired as I felt I could sleep for a year. I did sleep all the day long. Mrs. Russel brought my supper, but I would rather "sleep than eat." We did not hear of the terrible tragedy at Hegben Dam until late Tuesday. The events and deaths to the west of us were awful and overshadow any other incidents relative to the disaster.

Mr. and Mrs. Culligan returned to the scene Wednesday. It was simply edifying the manner in which they took their heavy loss. "It's God's will," said Mr. Culligan. "What He does is agreeable to me." Mrs. Culligan re-echoed her husband's sentiments. What an example of faith, trust and stability! God love them!

Not much more to say. Mr. and Mrs. Culligan left for Bozeman that afternoon. I accompanied them. On Thursday night I boarded a train for my monastery home in Richardton, North Dakota, where I am now.

Just a final word. By some quirk of fate I seem destined to be in on recent cataclysms. I was present at the terrible flood in Marysville and Yuba City, California, in 1955. I have been in other minor catastrophes and now this quake. Maybe it will be a cyclone next, or better I may learn to at least stay home. Well, whatever is in store for me, I hope I can face it as did Mr. and Mrs. Culligan in this last disaster — "What God wills is all right by me."

BLARNEYSTONE RANCH

Running through the Culligan ranch in the State of Montana flows the beautiful Grayling Creek — a sparkling, bubbling, rippling stream of life-giving soft aerated water, loaded with the energy of the sun. This stream has been flowing for centuries. It flows constantly, rapidly and joyfully. All children love it. It empties into Hegben Lake, which, in turn, overflows into the Madison River and on to Three Forks where the Madison, Jefferson, and Gallaten rivers consolidate their waters to form the mighty Missouri. This great river flows through the midwest for over two thousand miles to join the Mississippi at St. Louis, and together our two mighty rivers flow on to the sea. The water that once gave life to the much-sought-after Grayling mountain trout, on this ranch, finishes its active, useful, short life when it empties into, and forever becomes a part of the immortal ocean.

In the spring of the year, the Grayling overflows its banks to feed a swamp without an outlet. The same life-giving water in the creek when trapped in the slough becomes stagnant, odorous and lifeless. Travelers avoid the road that passes near it. No birds light upon it. No fish swim in it. Even elk and moose avoid it, for it is hoarded water, and it carries the odor of death.

In the beautiful Hegben Lake nearby — filled with the same water from Grayling Creek — fish of many varieties abound. In the fall millions of Canadian ducks and geese stop for a few days to enjoy this refreshing water on their flight south. On the banks, trees and greens of many species spread their branches, giving glory to God. Along its shores are summer homes of people from all America who travel great distances to enjoy this freshest of mountain water while fishing for mountain trout.

What makes the difference in these two neighboring waters? The swamp keeps every drop it receives. It is shrewd. It conserves all its income jealously. It gives nothing, for it has not the grace to give. It is a hoarder — a miser.

But Hegben Lake freely gives up its water. It uses only what it needs for the day. It is constantly giving as much as it receives. It hoards nothing. Its sparkling water laughs in the sunshine, and every kind of life rejoices. Hegben Lake gives and lives.

And so it is with God's providence in the hands of man. The man who gives as he receives — the man who takes and uses what he needs and passes on all else to help carry on God's plans for this world — that man, like the Lake, gives — and lives. His prayer is a simple, "Give us today our daily bread." The man who locks up God's providence in a tall building behind 20 ton steel doors and demands that his hoarded wealth glorify its creator and momentary owner, that man, in many ways, resembles the swamp.

PEACE ON EARTH

High in the Rocky Mountains we wanted to build a little settlement where materialism could not exist; where money, power, and wealth mean nothing. We invited a priest to live near us, a retired Army Chaplain, veteran of two world wars. He wanted a retreat somewhere on earth where he could say his breviary alone and be at peace, until our Lord called Him. He found such a spot at the Culligan ranch in a pine forest on the banks of a beautiful lake in the Sierras. He joined us and settled down to await the great adventure of the Beatific Vision. But such a man, even when incognito, could not hide from his neighbors the living Christ that dwelt vitalizingly within him. All unconsciously he "put on the Lord Jesus Christ" so that his neighbors almost mistook him for Him. He brought people of many faiths to Christ by merely being their neighbor, even though in the early days in the settlement he never spoke about Him. He considered his life work finished when the second war ended and, too, he was getting old. He desired to be a contemplative the rest of his days.

All neighbors soon loved this stranger, and seven families adopted him for a dinner guest one day a week. The children enjoyed hearing his stories of adventure, his recitation of poems, and his singing of Irish ditties. It became known that he was a retired General of the American Army. No one yet knew he was a priest. After several months he proposed to each of his seven beneficiaries that they pray together after dinner. He suggested the Rosary. He told beautiful stories of the Mother of God and of her visits to earth, especially of her visit to Portugal in 1917. The evening Rosary became an institution and soon many neighbors would gather for evening prayer wherever the General was dining. Months later, he suggested that all come to our chapel for Sunday morning prayer. He then told them that he was a retired Army Chaplain and a Catholic priest. He said he wanted to offer mass for all present. He explained what mass was. He told them that on the night before Christ died He took bread into His hands, blessed and broke it, and gave it to His disciples, saying: "This is my body." He told them the Blessed Sacrament is Christ — the whole Christ. He explained that when he was ordained a young priest, he was given the same power that Christ gave his disciples that evening — to continue to consecrate and distribute the whole Christ to all those who desired to receive Him. He explained that all members of the Catholic Church were part of Christ's Mystical Body, and that those receiving His Body became a living part of Christ Himself. And the people in the mountains believed what he told them.

Under the loving direction of this man of God, many of the neighbors joined the General's religion. Even without effort or study, man tends to fall in love with God; for the knowledge of His existence is written in the hearts of all men. Primitive man knows and responds to God.

Before the long "snowed in" winter was over, many persons in the settlement were daily receiving Christ in the Eucharist. Some visitors, sensing the peace and joy of the year-round inhabitants, decided to give up city life, too, and stay in the mountains. Before the next winter was over, perpetual adoration was conducted day and night by a community that two years before consisted of members of various religions.

The people found joy that comes with daily worship and reception of God Himself. They experienced the natural ecstasy and delight in the response of the senses, which are transformed into the very joy of Christ. Actually, as a part of Christ's Mystical Body, all these Christian people became Christ. To give the Holy Eucharist to such people morning after morning, was to lead the spiritually hungry to the royal banquet, which is the best way, if not the only way, to change ordinary people to living saints. This is what the General brought to a small settlement in the depth of rural America.

Only real men and real women fall in love with the quiet and stillness of the long winter where seven foot snow and forty below is routine. If the summer tourists find these mountains beautiful, they should see them in the purity of their winter snow. Only those who have seen immaculate mountain snow and spent winter days in such a retreat will understand.

Ex-city folks who had been disgusted with the materialism of the Twentieth Century — while searching for they knew not what — piling up money, honors, and things, found at this little haven of peace that possessions of adornment were not necessary; that actually in the settlement they were worse than useless, for they cluttered up the cabins. Money, too, was not needed in any sizeable amounts, for there was little that need be purchased. Foodstuff and fuel were taken off the land, out of the forest, and from the mountain streams and lakes. The mountains abounded in a great variety of fish and game. The land grew unbelievably large vegetables which both men and women enjoyed to harvest. All this was free. The game that the city man travels great distances to obtain on a two-weeks vacation, these natives had the year around at no expense. Homemade bread again became a woman's art; it was their greatest joy.

Thus, out in the great West, all unplanned, a group of American people of many faiths gave up the materialism of the Twentieth Century for the daily reception of the Body of Christ. Here, with Christ and His Mother, in the depth of the Rocky Mountains, true peace was found. Here, One Fold and One Shepherd was already a reality, as Christ and His Mother wish it to be for all everywhere. Here in the quiet of the mountains, and the cold of the winter, these good people found, like the Trappist in the silence of his monastery, that heaven can begin before life is ended.

OTHER TITLES AVAILABLE

St. Joan of Arc. Beevers.
Mary, Mother of the Church. Ripley.
Treatise on the Love of God. St. Francis deSales.
Purgatory—Explained by the Lives & Legends of the Saints. Schouppe.
Life of the Blessed Virgin Mary. Emmerich.
The Church Teaches—Documents of the Church. Jesuit Fathers.
Catholic Prophecy—the Coming Chastisement. Dupont.
Imitation of the Sacred Heart of Jesus. Arnoudt.
Wife, Mother & Mystic. Bessieres.
Life of Jesus Christ & Biblical Revelations. 4 vols. Emmerich.
Humanum Genus. (On Freemasonry). Pope Leo XIII.
Where We Got the Bible. Graham.
St. Pius V—His Life, Times & Miracles. Anderson.
Incorruptibles. Cruz.
St. Francis of Paola. Simi/Segreti.
Humility of Heart. Bergamo.
Chats with Converts. Forrest
St. Gertrude the Great—Herald of Divine Love.
The Incredible Creed of the Jehovah Witnesses. Rumble.
What Catholics Believe. Lovasik.
Is It a Saint's Name? Dunne.
Dogmatic Theology for the Laity. Premm.
St. Therese, the Little Flower. Beevers.
Second Latin. Scanlon.
Latin Grammar. Scanlon.
Three Ways of the Spiritual Life. Garrigou-Lagrange.
Dogmatic Canons & Decrees.
Rosary in Action. Johnson.
Religious Liberty. Davies
Convert's Catechism of Catholic Doctrine. Geiermann.
Glories of Mary. St. Alphonsus Liguori.
Life of Anne Catherine Emmerich. 2 vols. Schmoger.
Spiritual Conferences. Tauler.
Abortion: Yes or No? Grady.
Father Paul of Moll. van Speybrouck.
Holy Shroud and Four Visions. O'Connell.
Cure D'Ars. Trochu.
Story of the Church—Her Founding, Mission & Progress. Johnson
Uniformity With God's Will. St. Alphonsus.
St. Anthony—Wonder Worker of Padua. Stoddard.
Prophecies of St. Malachy. Bander.

Order from your bookdealer or directly from the publisher.

OTHER TITLES AVAILABLE

Book of Destiny. Kramer.
Evolution Hoax Exposed. Field.
The Secret of the Rosary. St. Louis deMontfort.
Mystical Evolution. 2 vols. Arintero.
Douay-Rheims Bible.
Begone Satan. Vogl.
Soul of the Apostolate. Chautard.
Dialogue of St. Catherine of Siena. St. Catherine.
Way of Divine Love. Menendez.
Brief Life of Christ. Rumble.
Stigmata & Modern Science. Carty.
Blessed Eucharist. Mueller.
Purgatory & Heaven. Arendzen.
Baltimore Catechism #3. Kinkead.
Hidden Treasure—Holy Mass. St. Leonard.
History of Antichrist. Huchede.
Who is Padre Pio?
Why Squander Illness? Rumble & Carty.
Bible History. Schuster.
Child's Bible History. Knecht.
Fundamentals of Catholic Dogma. Ott.
Meditation Prayer on Mary Immaculate. Padre Pio.
Agony of Jesus. Padre Pio.
Devotion to the Infant Jesus of Prague.
New Regulations on Indulgences. Herbst.
Prophets & Our Times. Culleton.
Reign of Antichrist. Culleton.
Christ's Appeal for Love. Menendez.
Pere Lamy. Biver.
Thirty Favorite Novenas.
Beyond Space—A Book about the Angels. Parente.
Padre Pio—The Stigmatist. Carty.
Catholic Catechism. Faerber.
Is There Salvation Outside the Catholic Church? Bainvel.
Life & Glories of St. Joseph.
Sacred Heart & the Priesthood. Mother Margaret.
Last World War & the End of Time. Culligan.
The Priest, Man of God. St. Jos. Cafasso.
Little Book of the Work of Infinite Love. Mother Margaret.
Open Lesson to a Bishop. Davies.
WayFinders. Plewe.

Order from your bookdealer or directly from the publisher.